William Cowper Prime

Along New England Roads

William Cowper Prime

Along New England Roads

ISBN/EAN: 9783744724869

Printed in Europe, USA, Canada, Australia, Japan

Cover: Foto ©Andreas Hilbeck / pixelio.de

More available books at **www.hansebooks.com**

ALONG
NEW ENGLAND ROADS

BY

W. C. PRIME, LL.D.

AUTHOR OF
"I GO A-FISHING" ETC.

ILLUSTRATED

HARPER & BROTHERS PUBLISHERS
NEW YORK AND LONDON

ILLUSTRATIONS

NO HOUSE WHICH DID NOT STAND IN A GROUP
OF TREES . . . . *Frontispiece*
THE CHURCH-BELL ANNOUNCES "EVENING
MEETING" . . . . *Facing p.* 22
A MOUNTAIN ROAD . . . . " 86
ON THE PROFILE ROAD . . . . " 124

PREFACE

PROBABLY no one ever made a book for the reason which induces the making of this. The papers here gathered were written, as letters, to a daily newspaper, the New York *Journal of Commerce*, in the course of a correspondence which has extended over more than forty years. Although often asked to gather them in a book, my judgment has been that such letters, however readable or unreadable when occasionally appearing in one's morning newspaper, are not good material for continuous reading in a solid book. They were written for the purpose of a day, served their purpose, disappeared, and I had no wish to recall them. But they had been cut out and preserved by more than one person, strangers to me, who have severally written me that if I do not make a book of them they will! Should such a book be made by another person, it would perpetuate many sad errors of type, such as occur in rapid newspaper work, and be a misfortune to the papers and to me. There was but one way to protect the dead and long-buried sketches—namely, to select some of them, revise, correct, and edit them, and make a book, which I have done only because I did not want it made.

CONTENTS

CHAPTER		PAGE
I.	ALONG NEW ENGLAND ROADS	1
II.	IN SOUTHERN VERMONT	17
III.	A VILLAGE DISCUSSION	34
IV.	UPHILL IN FOG	41
V.	SWEET-SCENTED FERN	45
VI.	AN ANGLER'S AUGUST DAY	54
VII.	VIEWS FROM A HILL-TOP	63
VIII.	HIGHLANDS OF WESTERN NEW HAMPSHIRE	70
IX.	THE TRIUMPHANT CHARIOT	77
X.	A DEAD LETTER	85
XI.	EPITAPHS AND NAMES	97
XII.	FINDING NEW COUNTRY	124
XIII.	BOYS WITH STAND-UP COLLARS	136
XIV.	PILGRIMAGE ENDED	143
XV.	NON-RESISTANCE	152
XVI.	SONGS OF THE AGES	160
XVII.	IGNOTUS	167
XVIII.	SEEKING A BETTER COUNTRY	175
XIX.	A WINTER NIGHT'S ERRAND	183
XX.	HINTS FOR CARRIAGE TRAVEL	190

ALONG NEW ENGLAND ROADS

I

THE carriage was standing at the door, and I had finished my morning inspection of horses, harness, bolts, and gearing. We were on one of our favorite journeys, wandering over the hills and through the valleys of New Hampshire and Vermont. We had driven already two or three hundred miles, seeking only that which we found daily, scenery, sunshine, birds, flowers, whatever of nature and whatever of humanity might be seen as we wandered along New England roads.

A gentleman who was standing in the hotel doorway said · "I am told you travel a great deal with horses and carriage. It puzzles me to know what pleasure you find in it. I have travelled in that way in Europe, but I don't understand what attractions you find in New England."

He expressed the idea which is in many minds. I could not afford to waste the morning in recounting to him the delights of carriage journeying. I gave him but a brief summary of these, told him there was no country in the world which was so charming to the traveller as this country, nor one in which scenery was more varied and beautiful, nor one in which country inns were so good, country people so hospitable, and finished by saying: "Try it for yourself, and if you don't enjoy it don't do it again."

The road was in that charming country which lies south of the White Mountain range. We had followed the Pemigewasset River from its source in Profile Lake, under the Old Man of the Mountain, day after day, until we had left it at Franklin Falls, and were now following our varying whims from valley to valley, over highlands and hills, through the very heart of the Granite State.

It was in May. The forests farther north had been just tinged with that delicious mauve color which is caused by the swelling buds of the maples, and which from day to day changes into pink and hazy sky blue and at length, when the buds burst, into green. But here the green had won the day, and the view in all directions, as I drove along, was fresh and full of promise. When the road led through forest both sides were luxuriant with the close-packed masses of ferns just commencing summer life, and in the woods were hosts of purple and striped blossoms of the trilium, the glory of our northern forests in the early season. I came out from a piece of woods on a plain where the road went straight ahead in full view for a half-mile. Nearly that distance ahead stood a farm-house, with its barns and out-buildings. The house stood back from the road among fruit-trees, some of which were in blossom. But what especially attracted attention was a large number of horses and wagons, vehicles of various descriptions, which made the front yard and the road near the house look black.

Only two events in the country life are likely to cause such a gathering around a house. When you see it you are quite safe in thinking that there is a funeral or an auction sale. Either is sure to bring together all the wagons of a very wide-spread population. There is this difference, however, that to the funeral men and women and children come, but to the "vandue" only men.

As I approached the house I began to pass horses tied to fences and small trees. Everything in the shape of a hitching-post, everything to which a halter could be tied, was in use, and when I reached the front gate there were groups of men so occupied here and there that no doubt could exist that this was an auction sale. It was undoubtedly a funeral in one sense, not of any one dead, but of a home. It was the extinguishment of a fire that had been burning on a hearth a great many years. It took but a little while to learn from those who were grouped near the gate the reasons for the auction. This group consisted of men who had come only because it was an occasion for meeting people, a chance for general talk and exchange of little news, a break in the monotony of country life. Near the barn was another group, inspecting cows. They had no interest in the sale of furniture in the house. On the front lawn was another group. I fancied they were discussing the value of the farm, whether it was worth the mortgage on it, whether any one was likely to bid on it. As I walked in towards the door I saw that there were people in all parts of the house, most of them in the large kitchen whence the voice of the auctioneer was audible. As I entered he was selling cooking utensils, getting from a cent to six cents apiece, rarely as much as ten cents for any article.

I confess that, as I looked around this kitchen on this scene, I felt very much as if it were a funeral, and began to think that I had an interest in, a personal acquaintance with the departed. It had been for a long lifetime the home of an honest, respected farmer, who had recently died; an old man whose work was ended. His children, all but one daughter, had gone to distant parts of the country. His wife had died a year before. The property must be sold to settle his small estate, pay his funeral expenses and perhaps other claims. There was to be also an attempt to find a purchaser for the farm, but it was thought the holder of a mortgage on it would be the only possible bidder.

That life was to be closed out forever. Wherein much of it had consisted was here visible. It was displayed for public view, and any stranger was free to rove from room to room and see the record, for nothing was reserved; not even the clothing, or the old man's silver watch, or his wife's work-basket with knitting needles and scissors, and a knife with a broken blade, and a ball of blue yarn and a half-knit woollen stocking.

Here was a summing up of the total reward in this world's valuables which a long, laborious life had earned. I can never cease to feel indignation at the preachers about labor and its rewards who imagine that workmen in the trades are the only laborers to be considered; who are deceived by the idea that the various societies of "working-men" represent one-tenth of the hard-working men of our country; who imagine that the labor question relates only to that small number of persons who work for fixed pay, eight or ten hours a day.

The life of this man from his childhood had been one of incessant labor, hard work, beginning daily long before daylight, ending so wearily after dark that he welcomed sleep as the only rest he knew. Your ten-hour city laborer does not know what work means, and never will know till he acquires a farm and has to support life by digging for himself, paying himself for his work, and finding that to the vast body of American farmers fourteen hours a day labor earns bare subsistence.

The life labor in this house and on this farm showed in the end, as the laborer's pay when all work was done, just nothing beyond the bare support of the life. Less, indeed, than that, for there was a mortgage on the farm, which represented a demand of some pressing need, or a steady, slow falling behind from year to year.

The home furniture was not luxurious; far otherwise. But it was not altogether without interest. There was an old chest of drawers in one room which probably belonged to the mother, possibly came from her mother when she was married. It was made of solid cherry-wood, and the old brass mountings were, for a wonder, brilliant as if new. There was a small looking-glass hanging on a wall, in a frame once of great beauty, the relief ornaments on it being ears of golden grain. There were some pictures in black-pine frames, without glass. None had any money value, but each had higher than money value, because they had been the delights of that family life. Children had grown up looking at them daily, their young imaginations wandering far away under the guiding influence of art. Mark you, my friend, art brings its blessings not alone by the power of renowned artists, by the works of great masters. There are very rude pictures, pictures which provoke the derision of ignorant critics, pictures which have had mighty influence in swaying human minds. There was a fifteenth-century artist in Cologne whose Bible pictures in rough hard outlines were the educators of millions of people for a century and more after he was dead. It is the thought written in the picture which is its power, not the execution, which is of account to very few who see it. There is no possible doubt that that old painted print of Ruth gleaning, and that other of the raising of the widow's son of Nain, had impressed lessons on young minds not to be effaced in this world's experiences, perhaps not in any other world.

The old kitchen seemed to be the place wherein the life had left its strongest marks. And yet they were not many. There was a little printed calendar of a year long ago pasted on the side of the chimney. There was a clock (not worth your purchasing, my friend) standing high up on a wooden shelf. There was a dresser whereon the family crockery was piled for sale. Having in mind friends who want old crockery, I looked over the pieces, one by one, but found nothing worth a stranger's purchasing, except, perhaps, one English plate with a blue print, the rich dark blue wherein the cheap Staffordshire wares surpassed all other,

Oriental or Occidental, potteries or porcelains. But the table was there, a very old square table, made of black-ash, with four solid legs. It had no claim to notice for any beauty about it. But around it the family had been gathered morning, noon, and evening. First the young man and his young wife had sat there alone, happy, hopeful. Years had fulfilled all they had hoped for, had brought little heads to the sides of the table, and years had changed them into older and perhaps wiser heads. All the troubles and all the happiness of every one of them had been brought to the assemblies at that kitchen table. Christmases, Thanksgiving days, wedding-days of daughters, days when the minister was to make his annual visit, all the gala-days of life had loaded the table with unusual feasts. And always with unfailing humility and gratitude, the voice of the father had been heard at the head of the board thanking God as sincerely as if the farm had been a gold-mine instead of slow-yielding soil.

I was in the house but a few minutes. As I drove rapidly down the road I overtook a man, going home from the sale. I am not fond of "buying bargains" in such cases. If there had been anything to tempt me I could not comfortably own a purchase out of that household at the poor prices things were bringing. But this man was carrying home something. As I turned out and drove by him he held it up for me to see. We went along side by side.

"What have you got there?"

"I don't know. I think it's an old pitcher they used in a church."

"What did you buy it for?"

"I don't know. I s'pose I can sell it to some one."

"How much do you want for it?"

"I don't know what it's worth."

"Well, speak quick, if you want to sell," and my horses were pulling ahead hard.

"I don't know as I care to sell it."

"All right," and I went ahead rapidly.

"Will you give two dollars?" came in a shout after me.

"Will you take it?"

"Yes."

He came up alongside of me and I took my purchase. It was never church property; quite otherwise. It was a fine, tall, old two-quart pewter mug with cover. It had done duty in times when men sat together while the pewter, filled with foaming beer, went around from hand to hand and lip to lip. It was in perfect order, but there was nothing about it which seemed in keeping with the old farm-house. When, four miles on, I stopped to feed my horses, the landlord, looking in my carriage, exclaimed, "Hello, did you buy Jake's pewter pitcher?" and then said Jake had bought it at another sale years ago, on speculation, and had carried it afterwards to every "vandue," trying to find a purchaser.

In the autumn of that year I drove again through the same country, sometimes on the same, mostly on other roads. The aspect of the hills and valleys was now very different. October is a golden month for carriage travel, on some accounts more pleasant than any other month in the year, both for horses and travellers.

The road passed through a forest, unbroken for half a mile. On the right a stream wandered over rocks, and under little bluffs of moss, bright green miniature copies of mountain bluffs along the courses of mighty rivers. Now and then, where the stream fell into a pool, the lower end of the pool was dammed with autumn leaves, yellow and red and brown, and in the whirl of the pool you could see the same colored leaves going around and around, and the water looked as if it were clearer and colder for their presence. The road was covered over with leaves, a yellow carpet, and every few minutes the light breeze would freshen up a little and shake the higher branches of the trees, and send down a shower of leaves, which flitted and darted to and fro, flashing in the sunshine, and falling on our laps and all around us.

At length the road, which going up a gentle ascent left the brook away in the woods, emerged into open country, and we found ourselves on the top of a hill. Before us spread one of those beautiful landscapes in which New England is richer than any other part of the world that I know of. The road descended into an oval basin, some three miles long and a mile broad, the bottom and sides of which were, or had been, cultivated farm lands, except where a small lake slept motionless. It was surrounded by low hills, up the sides of which the fields extended, here and there one of them glowing with the buff and gold of corn stubble and scattered pumpkins. Along the ridges, where the fields did not go over them, were groves of maple and birch whose autumn colors were intensely bright, while down the slopes lay many abandoned fields gone to brush, mauve, maroon, crimson, and purple-colored with their dense growth of bushes, scarlet-lined along the fences by rows of sumac.

If you can show me anywhere in the world landscapes which are as rich and varied in color as our northern landscapes in America, or which are more beautiful in the form and contrast of valley and hill, I will go far with you to see them. Autumnal foliage with many is thought to be the changed color of the forest leaves, and few have observed the wonderful painting of landscapes in the autumnal colors of the low bushes. Many of our New England rivers in October flow between banks and around low gravel islands which are unbroken masses of crimson from a plant not a foot high, covering every inch for acres. And the shades are even more beautiful than the intense colors, soft, rich, and delicate as old embroideries.

There was no village in the valley. As I drove along the road which led nearly through the middle of it I came, at a cross-road, to a graveyard and an old church. That it was once a church the remains of a tower or spire indicated, and its location, a hundred feet from both roads, in the graveyard, demonstrated. There had never been any fence around the lot except the rough-laid loose stone-wall which serves for fence in all parts of our country where stone is plenty. And no better or more picturesque fencing can be, especially if people will plant along such walls any of the many beautiful vines which abound everywhere, and thrive luxuriantly in just such places. But no vines had ever been planted here. Not a solitary bush or tree grew in the graveyard. Even grass seemed to have run out from lonesomeness and neglect, so that the ground looked like an old worn-out pasture lot, the only break in the desolate aspect being a stunted sprig of golden-rod which gleamed in front of the church door.

I passed it, careful not to tread on it, and tried the door, found it open, and went in. The interior was a sad ruin, through which the breeze was free to blow, for there was no glass in any window, nor, indeed, now any need of glass, since it was plain enough that there had not been for long time any assembling of people here to worship. The pulpit, nearly round and high up, backed by a large window, had once been reached by a winding stairway, now broken down. The pews, which were built of pine, without paint, were in fair preservation. The plaster on the walls and flat ceiling had mostly fallen off, and lay in the pews and on the floor of the aisles. I could see the blue sky through one great rift overhead where the roof timber had fallen in and crushed down the ceiling.

No places are filled with such profound interest to thoughtful men as those spots in which their fellow-men of former generations were accustomed to assemble for the worship of God. And places of Christian worship are more deeply interesting because of the characteristics of that worship which distinguish it from all others. In no other have men approached Deity with the sense of personal unworthiness which only their God can remove, and with faith in His fatherhood and brotherhood, His personal presence among them, and His love for them. From the early ages of the Christian Church this immediate and close relationship between God and man has been a distinguishing characteristic of old Christian art, whose earliest representations of His personality are as the Good Shepherd, carrying home a lost and found lamb of His flock. If that faith which directs their prayers be indeed the substance of the things hoped for, then the place where men meet their God is so truly the House of God that one is at a loss to understand those who deny any special sanctity in it. But however irreverent be their regard for the church which they themselves frequent, I think there are very few who can without some serious emotion enter an old church in which generations of men and women and children have worshipped, who are now lying in silent graves around it.

I don't think you, my friend, whatever your creed or your sympathies, could have sat with me in one of those plain pine pews, seeing the sunshine of that autumn falling through the shattered building on the ruined interior, and have failed to appreciate something of the sanctity of the old place of prayer. It was nearly noon. Through the broken roof one broad stream of golden light fell on the open place between the front pew and the pulpit. There the table used to stand which they called their Lord's table, and from which they received, as their catechism expressed it, "by faith," that is, by the highest assurance men can have, unhesitating belief, the body and blood of Him they worshipped. There, one by one, when the work and worry, the sorrow and sin of this life were ended, they were laid with closed eyes and calm faces, and thence carried out to the gathering place of the dead. Where are they now, strong men and matrons, young men and maidens, little children and patriarchs? As I asked myself the question I walked across the floor to a window and looked out. Yes, they were all lying there, as so many millions of the Christian dead all over the world lie, in circles that sweep over the surface of the globe, ever-widening circles as their faith has extended among men, all with their faces heavenward and their feet towards Jerusalem.

We spent more than a half-hour in the old church. I climbed by the wrecked stairway into the pulpit. Its interior casing was falling to pieces, and in a recess within were some scraps of paper, which had slipped between the boards from the shelf under the desk. On one was a memorandum of the minister for notices to be given of the weekly prayer meeting at Mr. ——'s house, and a Thursday night lecture at the school-house on the mountain. On another was a funeral notice. There was nothing else legible, except a torn scrap, the lower part of a leaf of a hymn-book, and on this was a stanza not unfitting the associations of the place. So for the moment I assumed the position of the erstwhile minister and said, from the pulpit, "Let us sing:"

"Oh what amazing joys they feel
While to their golden harps they sing,
And sit on every heavenly hill
And spread the triumphs of their King!"

There were only three of us, but one was leader of a choir in an up-country church; and we sang a good old tune, which, perhaps, they who were now silent around the church used to sing to the same words—and perhaps will some day sing again.

And while we were singing I saw a vision; not supernatural, but as lovely for the moment as any imagination. In the open doorway at the other end of the church was standing a little child, a girl of five years old, dressed in white, with masses of red-gold hair which the wind, coming in from behind her, was waving and shaking. Her great blue eyes were looking with wonderment while she listened. As the sound ceased she vanished. We might have thought it an apparition, but that, going to the door, we saw her running down the road as fast as her little feet would carry her, towards a large farm-house, nearly a half-mile off. Her story told at the house might have been the foundation of a mid-day ghost story for the neighborhood, the coming back of old-time people to sing an old hymn in the ruined church. But they could hardly suppose that ghosts would come in a travelling carriage drawn by a very solid pair of gray horses.

II

IN SOUTHERN VERMONT

It matters little which way you drive in Vermont to seek beautiful scenery. Every road furnishes it. The question each morning, which way we shall go, is not a very serious one. Ordinarily we ask about the roads in all directions, but not for the sake of getting information. That is hopeless. Few now have knowledge of a road to any place except the nearest railway station. At the station no one knows a road more than two or three miles away. This is not exaggeration. It is simply the result of the abandonment of carriage travel and the universal use of the rail. Intercommunication between outlying farms and villages is nearly at an end. The old social intercourse and mutual dependence of the country folk is mostly gone. The fathers and mothers knew every family within a circuit of ten or twenty miles. There are not so many families in the circuit now, but many have ceased, in this generation, to be even acquaintances one with another.

Night after night, sitting by the fire in the tavern

public-room, with ten or fifteen of the neighbors gathered for the evening talk, we have inquired about adjoining towns and roads thither, whether there are inns, whether the roads cross mountains, whether there are streams, ponds, lakes, which way and whither the watercourses run, but all in vain. And at the same time these men discuss with ample intelligence the Irish land question, the position of the French in Africa, the last news from Ethiopian explorers, and the politics of the United States. We seldom hear home politics talked about.

From all this you may infer that a ride through Vermont and New Hampshire is a journey of discovery. We go by inquiring almost from mile to mile. A good map, already marked over and over with the lines of our old routes, lies on the carriage seat. We start like a ship and lay our course by compass, or rather by the sun, for some place which on the scale seems to be at a reasonable distance, and ask from time to time whether we are on the right road. Occasionally we go wrong. It is of no account. We keep on, and arrive somewhere.

In the spring a trout rod lies ready for use in the carriage. In the autumn, a heavier rod and a gun. Here and there along the road are tempting spots for the angler, and I stop the horses awhile. In the forest roads, covered with fallen leaves and nuts in autumn, partridges are often to be seen, sometimes to be shot. Always the scenery is attractive. Comparisons of scenery are usually absurd. No two landscapes possess all of the same characteristics. One lake is unlike another, and it is impossible to compare one with another, except when the characteristics are so diverse that it may be fairly said of one or the other that it possesses little or no beauty. Mountains have their peculiarities, and one can seldom be intelligently placed in comparison with another as to the general quality of its scenery. One is bolder, grander, another is richer in lofty masses of color, and another has wonderful outlines of form against the sky. But, with some experience, I know no country which, as you drive through it, presents more variety of beauty, more rapid changes in the character of the beauty, more alternations of grandeur and pastoral calmness, more wild ravines, and more far-distant views, than Northern New England.

Proposing a wandering drive along the Green Mountains, I sent my horses to Brattleboro' as a starting-point. While waiting there for a friend I drove in various directions around the town. One could pass a month in Brattleboro' and drive every day a new road, and a good road, every rod of which is beautiful, whether in Vermont or across the river in New Hampshire. Streams pour down a dozen valleys between high hills, some cultivated to the summits, some forest-covered. Wild-flowers were out that spring in an abundance that seemed to surpass all former springs. The forests along the road-sides were luxuriant with thousands of flowers of a hundred varieties. The lateness of the spring had kept back the usual growth of early May, and the sudden coming of a succession of warm days had brought out the later and the earlier flora together. A mile out of the village there was a spot which was superb. Masses of violets grew as thick as pansies in garden beds, the large tall white and pale pink in clumps with the equally tall and large yellow, the small white and small yellow, and two varieties of blue, all intermingling and covering the ground at the edge of the forest, formed a continuous bed of color stretching a hundred rods with scarcely a break. Trilium, purple and painted, nodded over this bed in the deeper shadow of the woods now just leafing out. Anemone, tiarella, mitre-wort, were abundant.

Coming recently from watching the advance of spring in the South, the contrast was vast and striking. The luxuriant green over the whole surface of the country, ground and tree alike bursting out in splendid color, had not been a feature of spring in Florida and South Georgia. Last year's vegetation does not stand up here, dry and yellow, to be slowly hidden by the growth of this year, as in southern countries. Snow is a wonderful beautifier. It packs down the dead growth of the past, so that the first show of the new growth is visible and colors the earth and the landscape. There is a day when all the country looks wintry; the next day soft green tints show in the damp hollows or on the southern slopes; then in one or two or three days the whole landscape has become brilliantly green. The forests have begun to color. We all know the gorgeous autumnal colors, but little has been written of the exquisite tints of the spring forests in New England. They are often quite as beautiful as the autumn glories. They are softer tints, but more varied—pink, mauve, purple, and gray, in broad and gentle gradations, broken now and then by deep tints where the maple is budding. Sometimes in valleys, where willows are plenty and when sunlight falls richly after a shower, there are patches of golden yellow stretching across green fields which are as beautiful as one's golden dreams. Did you ever meet with one of those modern æsthetic maniacs who suggest improvements for Nature and criticise her minglings of color? One such condemns, as "in bad taste," the mingling of green with yellow in a field where thousands of yellow buttercups bloom. He suggests, as much more correct and pleasant to the eye, the contrast afforded by a midsummer field where the white daisies are abundant. There is no disputing about tastes. Nature offers something for every one; but that is a faulty education which has brought any one to apply to the works of the great Artist the arbitrary notions of what we call art criticism. Nature encourages no ideas of harmony in color. She mingles with a free hand all colors, and puts to shame the temporary and changing tastes of humanity, which trammel and harness artists and drive them on railway tracks of art production. Old nations of men are free from the foolish rules of so-called civilization in this matter of color. The gorgeous products and minglings of color which characterize the Chinese porcelains are doing a great deal to educate the dim and doubtful tastes of western Europe and America. The Saracens understood better than any race of men in any age the value of free and unrestrained use of color, and contrasted colors without regard to any ideas of what is called harmony. They decorated houses and temples as Nature decorates the earth, and kept prominent always the great lesson of the visible world, that with a blue sky and a green landscape every one of the infinite variety of hues of flowers is perfectly harmonious.

Taking Brattleboro' as a starting-point, we could cross the Connecticut into New Hampshire or strike out westward into Vermont. Choosing the latter course, we could continue the route northward on the eastern side of the Green Mountains, wandering hither and thither on the way, or take one of the roads westward and cross the mountains. What matters it which road you take? It is always easy

THE CHURCH-BELL ANNOUNCES "EVENING MEETING"

to turn your own carriage, change your direction, follow the new wish of the moment. We could go out to Wilmington, and over the Green Mountains to Bennington; we could turn northward from Wilmington and ascend and descend the hills of Dover, now getting far-off views over New Hampshire, now seeing to the west the Vermont mountains overhanging lovely valleys. The country directly west of Brattleboro', although hilly, abounds in fine scenery, and the valley at Wilmington is as lovely as any Swiss valley. We chose a route to the northwest. We drove out on the right bank of West River, following up the stream, with intent to spend the night at Fayetteville, but loitered along the way, and after sunset pulled up at a little inn in Williamsville.

There is seldom any trouble in finding employment for the evening at a country inn or in the village. Sometimes the church-bell announces "evening meeting," and one may do worse than to attend it, if only for the sake of seeing people and studying character. Almost always the inn is the place of gathering for some of the natives, who discuss all kinds of subjects with abundant intelligence, and generally with striking clearness and simplicity of thought and diction.

It is not difficult for a stranger to lead the conversation towards local incident and history. There is no country village in the land which cannot furnish personal histories of sufficient interest to make volumes of very instructive biography. You err if you imagine that only those lives are romantic which are passed among crowds in cities. The country life abounds in mysteries, romances. The clergyman or the doctor either could furnish the novelist with a great deal of material.

If you don't care to talk, you can always find on the table of the parlor, or on a shelf somewhere, a small stock of books; and if you are a reading man from a city you will be very sure to find these books mostly new to you—books you never saw or heard of. There are very few book-stores in New England outside the large cities. The New York or Boston publishers who sell books through retail stores have no means of reaching the inhabitants of Vermont and New Hampshire, except in two or three cities. The American people have not learned to any great extent to order books by mail. In the country few books are bought except such as are brought to the door by agents. For this trade a great many books are made of which no one in the cities ever hears. They are of various classes of literature, some of them good, instructive compilations of history, travel, scientific information, some only trash, catchpenny books. It is always good-fortune if one finds that the local history of the town or county in which he is resting has been gathered and published. Many such histories have been made in the north country. They are generally subscription-books, and special attention is given to the personal and family histories of subscribers. Portraits adorn them. Now and then ancestral portraits are reproduced in wood or lithographic prints. They are always readable books, especially readable for the traveller.

Williamsville is in the town of Newfane, a very old Vermont township. An excellent history of this town has been published abounding in material of much more than local interest.

In 1789, at the old Field mansion on the 22d of February, Major Moses Joy was married to Mrs. Hannah Ward, widow of William Ward. This William Ward had died insolvent, leaving debts of considerable amount. At the second marriage Mrs. Ward stood in a closet with no clothing on, and held out her hand to Major Joy through a hole, and the ceremony was thus performed.

This is the only instance I have ever met with in American history of what in England has been variously called a smock marriage, or a *marriage en chemise*. The idea was, and in parts of England still is prevalent, that if a husband takes a wife with nothing on her he avoids a legal liability to pay her debts, or the debts of a former husband, some of whose property she might possibly bring with her to her new alliance. This vulgar error has led to many curious marriages. One is recorded in which the woman left her room in the night, naked, by the window, standing on the top round of a high ladder, where she put on new clothes, and came down feeling satisfied that she had left all old obligations in the house, and come out scot-free. I think I remember in *Notes and Queries* an account of the surprise of a clergyman in an English church, when a bride appeared for an appointed marriage, wrapped only in a white sheet, and this within a very recent period. The old error, it seems, prevailed in Vermont so late as 1789, and Major Joy took what he thought the safe way of avoiding the responsibilities of the departed —and now not lamented—Mr. Ward.

There was another old error which also lingered in Vermont, according to the Newfane historian. Inasmuch as a writ was directed in words commanding the sheriff to take the body of the debtor, a common notion was held that the writ ran against that body living or dead. At a funeral in Dummerston, the adjoining town (no date is given), the officers arrested the body on its way to the grave. The procession stopped, the bearers gave bail for the appearance of the debtor, buried him, and paid the debt. In 1820, one Lee, in prison on a bail bond, died. The sheriff would not deliver his body to his family, fearing it would amount to an escape, and himself become liable. The consent of the creditors was obtained, and the sheriff, thus relieved from his apprehended responsibility, released his prisoner. This strange error was not confined to Vermont. Similar instances of arresting the body have been recorded in other parts of the country.

In the morning we changed our minds and turned south-westward. The drive from Williamsville to Wilmington is one to be remembered. A good road with a slight upward grade for four miles, then up a hill, through a small village, on for a mile; cross a bridge, up a steep hill, through Rock River village; still uphill through forest, the air pure and life-giving; uphill, uphill, a long steady pull to a church on a hill which is Dover Centre, and now behind us to the eastward there is no limit to our vision in the clear atmosphere which lies over New Hampshire. The blue horizon line away yonder must be almost where the sky and ocean meet. As we go on higher, the view seems to stretch yet farther into distance, east and northeast, and north, while close below us farms and valleys, hills and ravines lie as on a map. A half-mile beyond the church we cross the summit, and the western view of the Green Mountains bursts on us. And now we descend into a charming valley, and following a meadow brook which grows to be a river, and is the east branch of the Deerfield River, we reach Wilmington at noon.

It is a pretty village in a pretty valley. Hence

it is twenty miles to all sorts of places—twenty to Brattleboro,' twenty to Bennington, the same to Hoosac Tunnel and to Coleraine.

It may serve to show the freedom of carriage travel if I rapidly indicate the ways we went after this from day to day. From Wilmington we drove on southward and westward to Readsboro' City, a busy village among the mountains, at the junction of the east and west branches of the Deerfield River. Thence our route lay up the West Branch, a wild road of much beauty, to Hartwellville; then by a winding valley road to Stamford, and down to North Adams in Massachusetts; through the unrivalled scenery in which Williamstown is situated; down the Hoosac valley, and around a shoulder of the mountain to Bennington in Vermont; thence up the western side of the Green Mountains to Manchester. Northward now from Manchester, we drove up the beautiful valley between the high mountains on the east and Equinox and the Dorset mountains on the west, to Wallingford. There we turned the horses eastward again. From Manchester we might have taken a route west of the Dorset Mountain, by which we would have gone to Lake St. Catharine, a very lovely lake, whereon is a large hotel in a grove of pines. Thence the route is pleasant and generally level, with good roads, to Rutland, or to Castleton and on northward. I have often driven in this direction. But now, without any special reason, we recrossed the Green Mountain range.

The little highland village called Mechanicsville is in the town of Mount Holly, which includes the Green Mountain country east of Wallingford, where the hills run lower than to the northward and southward of it. The Central Vermont Railway line finds its way from Bellows Falls to Rutland across these lower hills in a north-westerly direction. The wagon road from Wallingford wanders in various beautiful ways. The pass across is one of the easiest and most practicable between the Massachusetts line and the gorge of the Winooski south of Mount Mansfield.

The carriage traveller may do well to make a note of these passes. If you drive northward from Troy or elsewhere on the west side of the mountains, you can cross them to the east side and the Connecticut valley only by one or another of these mountain roads.

From Bennington you can go over to Wilmington and Brattleboro' by a road which I have never happened to find in good order. From Manchester you can cross through Peru to Chester by a turnpike road, usually in fair condition. From Wallingford you can cross by the road I was now driving, to Ludlow. From Rutland you can cross by a road which I have found so wretched that the least said about it the better. From Brandon or Middlebury you can cross by good roads, that one which goes through Ripton passing the Bread Loaf Inn, and descending eastward to the hilly country south of Montpelier. North of this you can go through the mountains by a good road, with no serious hills, along the bank of the Winooski, to Waterbury and Montpelier. Still north of this you can drive over the rolling country around the north end of the mountains from Burlington to Hyde Park. There are other roads through and over the Green Mountains, but none of them can be recommended with certainty from year to year as practicable for pleasure carriages.

The morning was dark. We had had showers in the night, and the clouds still lay low in the valley at Wallingford. But a breath of air from the westward, slowly increasing, and beginning to move first the mists and then the leaves of the trees, gave promise of a clearing off. We did not start till late in the forenoon, and then the horses had four miles of pretty steady uphill work before them. A clear stream, swollen with last night's rain, roared down by the side of the road as we slowly ascended. There are doubtless trout in that stream, for along it now and then we saw boys fishing. None of them had any trout. All agreed that the water was too high, but all asserted the presence of trout. The faith of an angler is worthy the study of philosophers. If a boy knows that one trout has been taken in a stream, he will fish contentedly all day for another; and though he may take innumerable chubs and dace and minnows, without sight of the trout he seeks, he nevertheless throws in his bait a thousand times, and every time with perfect assurance that the next fish that takes it will have spotted skin and golden sheen below. So with all of us. They who know nothing about angling have few if any parallels in life to this faith, which is the underlying charm of going a-fishing. One cannot fish for long without success in a stream or lake in which he does not believe there are any fish. A few casts of the flies, a few minutes waiting for a bite at bait in this or that hole, and he abandons the place. But if he has seen a trout rise to a fly, or dash along the clear brook, it is enough. Thereafter faith takes hold of him, and the day goes on joyously to the end, even through he takes nothing. For the taking of fish is but a small part of the enjoyment of going a-fishing. The innumerable sounds and sights of nature, the luxury of open air, the clouds, the winds, the sunshine, the rain, the cutting off of thought of business, worry, care (which is cut off most effectually by the presence of the angler's faith in his rod and skill), these can be appreciated only by those who love to use rod and line.

We drove through East Wallingford and then wandered over hills, with many far and many lovely views until, on a hill-top, we entered the little village of Mechanicsville, consisting of a large factory, two churches, and a group of white houses under trees. The factory makes children's toys. It was startling, away up on the top of the Green Mountains, on the outlet of a small lake, to find a village supported by an employment so closely related to the home life of all the country. The forests of the neighborhood grow the wood, the mountain streams drive the saw-mills which rough-shape it, a steam-engine whirls the turning lathes and the various machines which give form to the objects. Here is another subject of thought for the philosopher. The angling boys were the morning illustrations of faith. The noon resting-place is a village where the inhabitants live by play. Nothing but play. The waters of a beautiful lake flow out over the factory wheels, working for play. Play clothes and feeds these families, enriches the manufacturers, supports perhaps these two churches whose spires rise side by side. It is a bright, cleanly, thriving-looking little village; the houses are neatly painted; the gardens are brilliant with flowers.

The frivolities of life have their uses. Children must play, ought to play; and grown men and women owe it to themselves to play sometimes. If you find any one who doubts the usefulness of play, tell him that it has its utility in this at least, that it runs a prosperous village in the Green Mountains, and employs a happy population with remunerative work.

In the afternoon our road led down the eastern slopes of the hills to the valley where Black River comes out from the succession of lakes at Plymouth and Tyson. We drove through Ludlow, and spent the night at Proctorsville. Next day we crossed the Connecticut into New Hampshire.

III

A VILLAGE DISCUSSION

I HAD pulled up at the door of a village store and gone in to make a purchase. I was standing at the counter. It was a cold day, and there were a half-dozen men sitting around the stove. All were strangers to me, for the village was out of my regular course of driving. I would have gone out immediately after making my little purchase, but that a remark from one of the men to the surrounding group interested me. It was made by a man whose face was bright and intelligent, but whose tone and style of talking marked him at once as somewhat dogmatic and given to laying down the law among his neighbors. I found afterwards that he was a young medical man, who had been but two or three years in the village, studious in his profession and remarkably successful, but fond of collisions with the Freewill Baptist minister, whose church was the only one in the neighborhood. The Doctor was an "educated man;" that is, he was a college graduate, and a man of some reading. The Minister was not an educated man, and the Doctor was a thorn in his side. Many localities in the country are situated much as this was. But, on the whole, the good-sense of the average man is superior to illogical reasoning, however specious, in or out of the pulpit, and sound orthodox belief holds its own against unsound reason and imaginary theology.

They were talking about miracles, and the young Doctor said: "You know as well as I do, Stephen, that everything in this world moves in regular order. The laws of nature are what we all have to depend on, and they never change. It's certain that if you plant potatoes they won't come up pumpkins. Neither you nor any man here ever saw a miracle. You never heard of one in your life in these parts. You never heard of pumpkin vines growing from potatoes. It stands to reason and common-sense that when no man in this town ever saw anything happen that wasn't in the regular course of natural law, anything supernatural, it isn't likely such things are going to happen here."

I looked at Stephen, as the Doctor called him. He was an elderly man, hard-featured and sunburned. There was a shrewd twinkle in his eye, but he looked at the stove and not at the Doctor, and there was silence for a moment while he pondered. Then he spoke in a mild, inquiring sort of way, which contrasted with the Doctor's somewhat self-opinionated tone.

"I don't know much about the laws of natur', but I suppose you mean something like this—that when I let go that jack-knife it 'll fall on the floor;" and he stretched out a long arm holding an open knife by the blade between his thumb and finger.

"Exactly," said the Doctor;" that's the law of gravitation."

"And it's sure to fall, and I can bet my money on it, and I needn't be afraid of a miracle? Look here, Doctor, where did the law that binds it to fall come from? What made that particular law?"

The Doctor was honest; that was evident from his reply. "The learned men who have investigated the laws of nature have not found the origin of the laws. They will in time. It's only in recent years that science has made its great discoveries in the laws themselves. Heat, light, color, electricity, all the great characteristics of the changing world and of matter itself, have never been understood as they are now."

"And you can't tell me what made the law that binds that jack-knife to fall down?"

"No, I can't. It's enough to know as certain that it will fall. Just let go, and you'll see the certainty."

"No chance of anything supernat'ral; any miracle?"

"Miracle be hanged. Let go the blade."

Stephen's thumb and finger separated and stood

stretched out wide apart. The jack-knife was not on the floor. It was hanging to the wooden ceiling overhead, its blade buried a half-inch in the soft pine. For about ten seconds no one spoke. Stephen was looking at the Doctor.

"Suthin' supernat'ral happened, didn't it?" said Stephen.

"You jerked the knife up yourself."

"Well, that warn't nat'ral, war it?"

The Doctor hesitated. "Now see here, Doctor," said the old man, "just tell me how old is your law that the jack-knife's got to fall down."

"Millions of years old. Just as old as there has been anything to fall."

"And how old was the law that said that jack-knife must go up there and stick its blade in that white-pine ceiling. Just three minutes and a half old by the clock. Now what I want to know is where did your law that it must go down come from. You say you don't know. Well, it stands to sense, then, and you can't deny that it may come from some one that makes it go down just as I made it go up. If your science is worth a sneeze it oughtn't to deny what it don't know nothing about. And if that's so, it's always just as like as not whoever made the thing go down will make it go up, without you or I or any one else knowing what made it go, any more than you know what made me jerk that knife up yonder. You tell me that if I plant potatoes they won't come up squashes, but you just tell me what plants potatoes, or what makes me plant 'em, anyhow. If I don't plant 'em there ain't going to be any potatoes nor squashes. It's according to reason that if potatoes come up because I planted potatoes, squashes don't come up from them, because some one else takes care of that part of the business. I don't believe in your argiments that laws always may be depended on, when you tell me yourself that you don't know where the laws come from and how long they're goin' to last. Your science is all right, Doctor, just as long as it talks about what it knows about. But when your science says a knife's bound to fall down, and don't take into account that something supernat'ral may interfere that science don't know nothing about, sich as my sudden making up my mind to jerk it up, why your science ain't wuth any more than a last year's almanac to tell a fellow what the weather's goin' to be."

By this time Stephen's tone and style had changed. He was no longer humble and inquiring, but decidedly aggressive. There were some strong words, not exactly profane, adjectively applied to science in the last sentence, which I have omitted. He talked rapidly and vehemently and with pointed logic. Is logic one of the distinguishing characteristics of humanity? There are men, exceptions, sometimes men of eminence, who do not seem to have any idea of logic, but by the vast majority of men, however uneducated, logical sequence seems instinctively appreciated, and the most illiterate are very sure to detect failure in argument.

As he talked he rose and stood up, six feet two —a mighty frame, fit for tremendous work—and he poured out a storm of plain and unanswerable philosophic truth, ending up in this wise: "No miracles, but only jest steady laws? Well, accordin' to law that jack-knife will stick there till the wood rots or the steel rusts. Make your prophe-cy if you dare. Say what it 'll do. Is there any law that 'll tell you what 'll come of it? or whether Sam or Timmy won't have it down and pocket it as soon as I'm gone? You don't know. Well, I do. There's just such a law, and I made it;" and so saying he reached up his long arm, seized the knife, and strode out of the door, growling as he went.

"He's a cantankerous old cuss, but he's got a lot o' brains," remarked one of the group. The others signified assent. The Doctor said nothing, but stood looking at the spot in the ceiling where the knife had been. I followed the philosopher. As I drove up the road I overtook him and offered him a ride. He had not noticed me at the store. He discussed my horses, the merits of various styles of buck-board, the weather, the crops, and it was not until we approached a farm which he pointed out as his own that any allusion was made to the discussion. There was a field golden with huge pumpkins, which I think form the richest and most gorgeous-looking crop that is ever seen in the fields. "You didn't plant potatoes for that crop," I said. He looked puzzled, then broke into a hearty laugh. "You see the Doctor riled me a little, and I got mad. I tell you what it is, Mister, I never had an edication, and the Doctor had; and it makes me mad when a man like him talks to a store full o' people as if he knew all he's a-talking about, when he don't. He's been going on about miracles for the last three weeks, because the elder preached a sermon on 'em. I don't belong to the meetin', but my old mother did. Do you see that bunch o' spruces over yonder? She's there. She believed in miracles. And she knew a heap more than I do. Now I just ask you this: which is best wuth believin', my old mother when she told me the miracles was true because there's a God over the airth, or these consarned edicated fools that go around saying there never could a-been no miracles because they don't know how to work 'em."

IV

UPHILL IN FOG

MAPS give little idea of the elevations or depressions in the surface of a country, except as the run of the watercourses indicates the slopes. The high mountains of Northern New Hampshire are generally laid down on all maps, but few persons have any idea that in the lower part of the State there is very high land, and that to reach it from the Connecticut on the west, or the Merrimac on the east, an ascent of more than 1000, perhaps more than 1500 feet, must be accomplished. I have no means at present of ascertaining the elevation of the highest farms in such towns as Lempster, Washington, and Stoddard. Some years ago, driving over the high farm country in Stoddard, I was told that this was the highest cultivated land in the State. This may be doubtful, but it is very high, and these towns ought to be above the hay-fever line. Judging from the experience of the direct pull up from Charlestown to Lempster, we should be inclined to think the latter village several thousand feet above the Connecticut. It was a magnificent ride.

The morning was foggy. October frequently fills the Connecticut valley with fogs. This was very dense and dark. As we went out from Charlestown and began the uphill journey, we came slowly into thinner mist, and after awhile into that most weird and solemn of all lights, the golden atmosphere of the October sun in fog among autumn forests. Stopping the horses on a water-bar for a little breath, we listened to the silence. Do you know what that means? It is not listening to nothing. There are sounds and many of them; but in the stillness of a foggy morning these sounds seem to cut sharply into the silence, and thus make you aware of the excessive stillness and calm which reign around you. The fall of a single leaf, broken off by the weight of moisture on it, is distinctly audible as it flutters to the ground. The voice of a crow, far away in the fog, comes through the yellow air with a metallic ring. You start along, and the crush of the wheels in the gravel is echoed from the side of the woods across a hollow, so that you think there is a water-fall over there. You stop again, and the echo dies away with a low murmuring along the trees, and the stillness is wonderful.

Uphill and downhill, but more and more uphill, the road mounts the high land. Ahead of us there are long views between the maples and birches, the view ending in yellow mist. We think that point must be the top, but when we reach it the road swings around the side of the hill and stretches on up. We descend at length, but it is into a hollow, and it grows dark and darker in the fog as we go down, till at the bottom, where a stream crosses the road, we think it will rain in five minutes, so deep is the gloom; but we go up again into the sunny mists, and at length, on a summit, feel for the first time a breath of air coming from the southward. When the air begins to move the fog will vanish. Its vanishing now is almost instantaneous. We have scarcely time to exclaim, "See that hilltop over yonder, and that one beyond, and this one, and"—far as the eye can reach, rolling away under the rich sunlight, lie the red-and-gold hills and the highland farms of New Hampshire. Patches of fog remain here and there and in hollows under the sides of hills, but they disappear in a few minutes. The view is so sudden and so vast that even my horses stop short and look at it.

But Lempster is still ahead of us, and we have yet higher heights to overcome. It was nearly twelve o'clock when we reached this little village— only four or five houses, with a new church and an abandoned old church. We had dinner, and then went over other heights to Washington. I do not know which stands the higher, Lempster or Washington. Both are attractive places, on account not only of their elevation, but also of their splendid surroundings of scenery.

Lovel Mountain is prominent near Washington. A farmer told me the legend of the origin of the name. I heard the story fifty years ago, and then believed it, as children believe, with ready faith. We grow sceptical as we grow older. But the farmer told it as a historic verity, and it is probably about as true as nine-tenths of what we call history. He believed it, and I don't know why you should not. A settler near this mountain in early times, named Lovel, was splitting rails, when six Indians surrounded him and made him their prisoner. My informant was sure of the number—there were six. The settler agreed to go quietly with them if they would wait till he finished splitting the log he was at work on. They consented. He adjusted his wedge in the long split, and induced them to take hold of the two sides to hasten matters by pulling the log apart. Then knocking out his wedge, he caught their twelve hands tight and fast in the spring of the closing split, and applied his axe, seriatim, to the six heads. The result was six dead Indians, and the later result the name Lovel Mountain.

V

SWEET-SCENTED FERN

THERE can be no reasonable doubt that the sense which is most closely linked with our powers of memory is the sense of smell. We are greatly puzzled sometimes to know what has suddenly brought to mind an event of long ago, a person whom we have not thought of for years, a scene that has been forgotten since childhood. Very often this sudden memory has been roused by a passing odor, the never-lost perfume of a flower, a handkerchief, a meadow. So subtle are the operations of the mind that we know little about them, and least of all about that stow-away place which we call memory. Neither you nor I know a hundred thousandth part of what we really do know, what we have learned, treasured, and now keep stored up; only it is like some things we have so carefully laid away that we can't find them when we want them, or have ceased to know that we possess them.

There was once a boy. It was a great while ago; that is, it seemed to him a long while to come, when he, a boy, looked forward to the old age he afterwards reached. But when he was an old man it did not seem such a great while ago that he was a boy, living in a small house, half log half clapboard, on the edge of a clearing in New Hampshire. This boy lived there very much alone; for though he had a father and a mother, it goes without saying that a small boy on a new farm leads a lonesome life when father and mother are at work all the waking hours. When he was ten years old he was a hard-working boy too. He had never been to school, never even learned to read. There was not a book, not so much as a Testament, in the house; and so far as he had ever heard, there were no books in the world, nor any God in it or over it. I wonder if you know, what is the solemn fact, that there are families, American families, with one, two, and many children, in New England States, of exactly this description.

Another family came into that part of the country, and another small house went up on the opposite bank of the lake; for the houses stood on a pond, or lake, which was a half-mile broad and two or three miles long, and the old forest was all around it except for the two clearings. Now came into that boy's life a new light, and he began to know the world; for there was a daughter in the other family, besides two sons; and what cannot a boy learn of the world from two other boys and one happy little girl. He learned more from her than from them. For somehow he learned from her to look into himself, and think about himself and what he was. That is a long step towards knowledge of the world when a boy gets into the way of studying himself thoughtfully. For almost all the joys, ambitions, and enjoyments; almost all the sins, labors, and sorrows of mature life are miniatured in the boy life. The little pleasures of the child are like in character to the great pleasures of the man. The triumph of a successful attack on a woodchuck's hole is the far-away antetype of a great operation in stocks or the brilliant capture of a large corporation.

Many a summer evening when his work was done he paddled his dug-out across the pond, and he and she drifted along the shore, and he sat silent while she told him stories of the town in which she had lived, and the people in that (to her) great assemblage of humanity. Many a Sunday they wandered together in the woods and out in the clearing along the bank of the lake, brushing through thick masses of fern that filled the sunny atmosphere with delicious odor.

After the first few months of their acquaintance, when he was twelve and she was ten years old, he had begun to regard her as the dependence of his life, and so to look to her for help. It was hard work to bring himself to confess to her that he did not know how to read; but he did it, and asked her to teach him. There was a rock among the sweet-scented fern by the shore, where in the pleasant Sunday mornings she gave him regularly a four-hours' lesson. She was not long in teaching him all she knew, and after that they progressed together.

They talked much and thought much. She told him Bible stories, and they were about the only stories she knew except two or three wonderful fairy stories which he and she mixed up with the Bible stories, until they grew wiser, as new settlers came and brought books, which they borrowed. Much they learned out of their own heads, reading together and giving each to the other, in childish wise ways, their deductions and reasonings about things visible and invisible, things of earth and things unearthly if not truly heavenly. Do you imagine their deductions were worthless? Nay, the ratiocinations of a boy and a girl about the infinite and invisible are about as valuable in result as are those of many of the philosophers which fill the thousand pages of modern books. They learned as much of final truth as you can learn from all the metaphysicians.

It needs not to say that he learned the old lesson of love at the same time, or even before he learned his letters among the ferns. So began his life. At seventeen he came out from his wild home into the crowded world. There is no space to tell of his method of farming his new farm. He went at it with the experience of the boy who had cleared a forest and rolled rocks out of the meadow land. It was a terrible piece of work, begun with semi-starvation, carried on with slow, steady determination. Starting as a day-laborer, he achieved in six years or so a superintendent's position with a living salary. Then he went back to the old farm and married Harriet, who had waited for him, and brought her to the city.

Fifty years went along, and neither he nor she ever again saw the north country. He accumulated property, and they were good members of their social circle, regular in daily life and Sunday churchgoing. They had changed, and yet had not changed. Their young lives had been devoid of romance, and there was no romance or sentiment in growing rich or growing old. Practically they had forgotten their youth. Certainly they never thought or talked of it. I said their youth was without romance. Yet beyond doubt the forming period in their lives had been when the unspeakable beauty of a boy's and a girl's love hallowed those sunshiny days. They did not know that there was any romance in young love on the silver lake in the mountain moonlight. They did not know there was any romance when he lay in the ferns at her feet and listened while she taught him that b-o-y spells boy and g-i-r-l spells girl and l-o-v-e spells love. Therefore there was no romance about it. It was simple matter of fact. They lived matter-of-fact lives when poor, and the same when rich and when surrounded with all the luxuries and elegancies which great wealth commands. They lived, in short, very much as many rich people live who have few resources for mental occupation, who are not given to much reading or much thinking—in fact, just living along, and keeping at the old daily routine of employments. There are many who live in this way, having neither past to enjoy in retrospect nor future to enjoy in prospect, only comfortable in the monotonous present.

He was growing feeble. His brain was weary or worn. It hurts the brain to use it forever on one line of employment. His had been used for nothing but business work now a half-century, and whether in memory, judgment, or looking to the future, no thought had occupied it except thought of property, buying and selling and getting gain. He had not for years been at three minutes' distance from a telegraph-station. His idea of a summer vacation was to go to a hotel where stock bulletins were always kept up, and stock operations were the day and evening subjects of discussion. No wonder that there came a time when he began to grow strangely silent, sometimes as if drowsy, sometimes morose. Then he suddenly seemed to forget everything, and neither spoke nor wrote, nor went to his private telegraphic instrument; for he had made his house an annex to his office and the Exchange, and had lived practically day and night in the street.

They said his brain was done with work, and his end was near. Still he walked and rode around, but never alone. One day he was riding with his wife in the carriage along an up-town road, silent, unobservant, apparently in a stupor, when suddenly he exclaimed, "How sweet the ferns smell in this sunshine, Harriet." She turned to him, and saw that his eyes were closed. She took him home, and after that he lay, week after week, quiet, but apparently without knowing or noticing anything or any one. But sometimes they saw a smile spread over his pale face, as if pleasant thoughts were in the old brain. After months of this, one evening in the twilight he reached out his hand to her and said, "How sweet the ferns are, Hattie." Then he seemed perplexed about it, and said, "How sweet the ferns were, Hattie," and then after a little he came into his right mind.

If in the other life, which is alongside of this our life, close to us, but invisible to us, there are, as we are taught by some serious teachers, angels appointed to each of us, who are sometimes able to influence our thoughts, it would seem sometimes as if those angels held in their hands the ghosts of things that are gone, the shades of our lost objects of delight, and somehow made us sensible of their nearness. Did his angel and her angel hold in their hands fragrant ghostly ferns gathered long ago, with subtle odors, sensible not to the actual sense, but quite so to the mental sense? Or did they bring fronds that grow in elysian fields, which bear odors like those that are here associated with our purest recollections? Why not? There are rivers there, and why not golden-rod on their banks, and fragrant mints and ferns? It must have been from heaven, with attendant benediction, that the odor of the ferns came often to him. For now they two, old man and old wife, lived again together for many weeks and even months the young life. All its old unrecognized romance and all its ample delight and happy peace of mind came back to them. They talked now of every tree and rock and flower-bed, of every odor of field and forest. You know we cannot describe an odor; we can only say how sweet or disagreeable it was; but always their saying was, "Do you remember how the air was full of the fragrant everlasting that September day when we did so and so?" and they talked over the old stories; and now she found them in books and read them to him, and the truth that was in them seemed very true. For were they not both rapidly nearing the world whereof they had talked so much and thought so much, and were they not soon to see Moses and David and Zaccheus and Bartimeus? For a year or more they were as happy as two children, happy as they had been when children; happier, I think, for their old hearts went rioting around in the memories of those days, and all the pains of them were gone. Once in the summer-time he said he wished when he should be dead she would send and get a great deal of sweet-scented fern and cover him with it. And she did so. And two or three years after that she died. Do you believe there will be ferns in heaven, sweet ferns, whose odors fill the air and help to memories of young life here? The old song of the Church says, "There cinnamon and sugar grow, there nard and balm abound." If they reach heaven, and ferns grow there, they two will be found often on some fern-bank. To them that would add much to what Gregory called "the sweet solemnity of those who are come home from the sad labor of this wandering."

VI

AN ANGLER'S AUGUST DAY

It was late in the afternoon of a superb August day, and I had yet some fifteen miles to drive, all the way over hills, and the last three miles up the mountain. I was driving the black horses, heavy animals, but swift devourers of mountain roads, rushing up hills and going down them with sure steps.

I had been far down the western valley, fishing a magnificent stream which is seldom visited by anglers, and has in it a goodly stock of trout. It is not to be supposed that in this hot month one can take a large basket of fish in any lake or stream, unless the weather be exceptionally favorable. And this day had been by much too bright. Nevertheless I had accomplished all that could be desired, all that any sensible angler has right to desire. I had strolled a mile or more, sometimes in, sometimes alongside of a glorious torrent, wandering its ancient way through primeval forest, down the last slope of a mountain ravine. My basket was not full, but there were a couple of dozen of fair-sized fish in it, and some dozens of smaller and more toothsome trout; for to my taste the only trout which equal fresh sardines in delicacy and flavor are the little fellows, from clear cold waters, which, fried brown and crisp with good salt pork, you take by their tails in your fingers and eat bodily, to your gastronomic satisfaction.

The road now led along a flat stretch of wooded country and came out in a clearing, where has been for more than thirty years a small saw-mill. A stream, rising in a swamp a mile or two above the mill, is dammed at the road-crossing, and sets back a small pond of two or three acres, mostly shallow, except where the old bed of the brook winds through it. The pond was a mirror in the now reddening light of the sun which just rested on the ridge of a tree-fringed hill to the westward. A small boy was standing at the road-side, looking at the water. Oddly enough he recognized me, as having more than once met me on streams in the neighborhood. "Oh, mister!" he shouted, as he saw me, and ran towards the buck-board. Of course I pulled up.

"There's a buster of a trout in the pond this year. You can see him walloping around every day just about this time. There he goes now. Isn't he a slosher?"

Up at the head of the pond, where the stream came in, there was a great swash in the water, and the waves which rolled away in a circle indicated a heavy animal of some sort.

"Isn't it a musk-rat?"

"No, sir," with emphasis on the last word. "I've seen him go two feet up into the air more times nor you can count. He mostly stays up there. But he won't take no worm nor grasshopper. Last June father tried him with a white grub, but you see its shaller water up there, and we can't get nowhere near him with the raft without scaring him."

"Where is your raft?"

"Down there by them willers."

I handed over the reins to my driver and took my rod. It was ready for instant use. I never drive in this country without a rod in the wagon, and when actually off for a day's fishing I do not take the rod apart until I have left the last possible angling places behind me for the day. There were two flies on the leader, which was stout, for fishing a rough river. They were not flies likely to be of any use on a still pond; so I put on a gossamer leader, with two small gnats for bobbers and a small white moth for the tail. It was early for the moth, but as it was already on the leader in my fly-book I did not change it.

The raft was a boy's, built for some seventy-five pounds of humanity to float on. Two hundred weight was almost too much for it, and it sunk one or the other end as I balanced myself on it, standing in my rubber boots with a varying depth of water swashing over my feet. I poled out into and across the pond towards the inlet. The boy was right as to the swirl being that of a trout. As I pushed along carefully and looked ahead I saw two similar swirls three rods apart. There were two of them then, at least, and possibly more; for now I began to recall the fact that years ago the owner of the saw-mill told me there were large trout in his pond which he could not take; but I then thought, from its shallow character, with muddy bottom, that he probably saw pickerel or some other fish, especially as the next owner a few years afterwards had told me there were no trout in the pond and no small trout in the swamp brook above it.

Did you ever pole a raft over a pond with soft mud bottom? No? Then you have never enjoyed the finest possible illustration of many scientific principles, action and reaction, the correlation and conservation of forces, the attraction of cohesion, innumerable interesting subjects of consideration, all of which would be pleasant to study if you were not occupied with your immediate purpose of getting across the water. There is a pleasant assurance of advance as you drop the end of the pole, push gently downward and backward, looking forward, and the pole passes through your grasp, renewed again and again, till the end is in your hand and you hold on to draw forward for another shove. But you can't draw it forward. It draws you backward, and the heavy raft, moving almost imperceptibly, has yet, with your added weight, sufficient momentum to go forward with your feet while your hands remain stationary, and you turn around, desperately grasping one end of the pole whose other end has gone down deep into the tenacious bottom mud. It went down so easily, gently, softly, that while you thought you had pushed your raft ten feet forward, you had only pushed your pole nine feet into the mud; and yet, lovingly as it went into the soft bottom, it refuses to return. Look out for yourself now. Hold on to the pole, or you will be adrift on the pond with no means of reaching shore. Hold on with your toes, with the soles of your boots, with your knees, anyhow you can, hold on to the raft. I have seen many an inexperienced man push his raft out from under his feet. I have done it myself in days of juvenile inexperience.

My raft was not a very heavy one, and the rule is to use your pole without deep pushing on such ponds, rather dragging, with the end only a little way in the mud.

I had followed the edge of the old bed of the brook, and with patience and perseverance came within a hundred feet of the place where the last trout had risen. There was no perceptible motion in the air, but there was a motion, nevertheless, such as anglers are familiar with, indicated by the fact that your cast goes out more easily with than against it. My rod was good for long casting, and I could lay the white moth-tail fly down within a few feet of the spot I desired to reach. I laid it down there a dozen times, and nothing else disturbed the surface, which now reflected a rosy cloud in the south-west. The sun had gone down. The original impetus given the raft and the existing movement of the atmosphere were carrying me slowly towards the mouth of the brook, which came out, a rod wide, between high banks covered with dense sedges. Up in the stream I saw three or four times the lift of a trout's head as he rose gently to the surface and took in some floating insect. He was feeding, August fashion, on some very small gnat, too small for imitation. So I tried approximation, changing the tail-fly, and for the white moth substituting a minute black object, the smallest lure known to my book, or any one's book, being a tiny hook, smaller than any regular number, tied with a yellow body and a delicate sparse black hackle, not an eighth of an inch long. I had drifted to the very mouth of the brook by the time this was ready, and the first cast sent it far up the canal-like stream. As it struck the water there was a magnificent roll of the glassy surface, a flash of reflected blue and crimson and pink and white in the water. It was as if some gorgeous piece of fireworks had burst on the dark surface between the sedge banks.

How many pounds of trout flesh and force were now on the end of that gossamer leader I shall never be able to tell you, for when he felt the slight stroke which fixed the tiny hook in his mouth, he made one swift, short rush, and I found that the leader was fastened on something heavier than a trout. There was nothing to do but break it loose or pole up the stream and try to unfasten it. I broke it, for I wanted another cast over that water. Half of the leader came home, with one fly yet on. I looped the end, put on another of the same small black hackles, cast three times; at the third cast again saw the brilliant explosion of the water-surface, again struck a heavy fish, and was again fast to something immovable.

This time I poled up to the spot. I might have hooked a hundred fish there and should never have gotten one. For my tail-fly had fallen each time just about ten feet beyond a great tree-trunk—a smooth, round log, two feet thick—of which the two ends were embedded in the banks on either side, while the log itself stretched across the stream about six inches below the surface. Under it the water was ten feet deep, and the fish had risen from this hole and plunged back into it, catching the upper flies in the log.

Twilight was established by the time I had put

on the small white moth which I proposed to use for the last few casts. You will observe that my raft would not go over the log, and I could go no farther up-stream. So I sent the flies up again and again and again, while the night gathered rapidly. Our twilights grow short up here in August. The air was ringing with the voices of frogs, with indescribable variety of tone and enunciation. The sharp cry of a night-bird in the air overhead pierced my ears. I saw a great Cecropia moth crossing the stream just beyond my cast, and a dozen smaller moths flitting over the sedges. Suddenly, behind me, a trout rose in the old place. I fixed the pole against the log, pushed the raft back, and dropped the tail-fly in the centre of the circle of waves. This time I struck my fish firmly, and he went for open water; it was an easy matter to bring him in; he was only a two-pounder. A two-pound trout is a small affair to the angler who has lost a four-pounder. And those two fish I lost were, of course, four-pounders—five-pounders; who can prove to me that they were not?

Whatever their weight, I was fully as content as if they were in my basket, which hung on my shoulder, or on the dry end of my raft if they were too large for the basket. I see your smile of incredulity, my friend; but you are one of the miserably uneducated community who will never appreciate the fact that the joy of the angler's day is in the surroundings of his sport. The very regrets he may have for lost fish are pleasant, not painful, if the day has been bountiful in the ordinary delights which attend the fisherman. My day had been exceedingly rich. As the horses came up the dark mountain road, guiding their own steps since I could not see to guide them, I recalled a score of beautiful scenes along the course of the mountain torrent, great bowlders lying in the foam, fern-covered cliffs, under which the river ran swift and smooth, giant white birch-trees on the bank, the outposts of armies of mighty trees behind them, rank on rank as far as eye could penetrate their array. And the dark lagoon-like stream, on which the twilight came down till the stars were reflected in it; the swoop of the nighthawks overhead; the call of the whippoorwill sitting on the saw-mill roof and the answer of his kin on the hill-side beyond—where can one close the catalogue of sights and sounds and thoughts, which made the hour's delay at the mill-pond a charming episode at the close of an angler's August day?

VII

VIEWS FROM A HILL-TOP

"HE was a very old man," said the landlord.

"How old?" I asked; "what do you mean by 'very old?'"

"Well, close on to ninety, I should say. No one exactly knew, and he didn't know himself. At least he said he didn't."

"He ought to have known a great deal."

"Well, it ain't always the man that lives the longest that learns the most. But Uncle Zekel did know a considerable deal. There wasn't a tree or a plant around here he couldn't tell you something about. There wasn't a square foot of land within ten miles that he didn't know everything that would or wouldn't grow on it. Then he understood the weather better than the newspapers nowadays, and he knew human natur' through and through. He never made a mistake in judgin' a man. He was sharp as a steel-trap when any one tried to come it over him. But he was so kind o' simple in his ways and his talk that strangers never thought much of him. Yes, he knew a great deal more than any of the rest of us hereabouts. Somehow everybody believed that he could see farther into a stone than any other man."

We were talking of an old man recently dead. It was at a way-side inn in Vermont, where I had stopped for the horses to feed and rest, and I was talking with the farmer-landlord, seated under a tree that shaded the front of the cottage-inn. Across the road, a little way below, there was a gathering at the door of a small house, which had led to the talk. The village people were coming together to carry to his grave the oldest resident, and while they were gathering the landlord told me about him.

No one now living remembered when he came to this part of the country. He was a Scotchman by birth, and though long practice had modified his voice and accent, there always remained in it some of the peculiarity which is musical to all who are familiar with Highland voices. He had been married in his early life, had children, and a household whose memories he sometimes, but rarely, referred to. All were gone. Wife and children had now lain side by side in the village graveyard for more than a half-century. All his friends of early life were gone as well. Most of them rested in the same safe enclosure.

Now this man's life was not, you will say, remarkable in anything. It was but the common life of man in the country, only a little longer than the average. You are right in this, that it was only an ordinary human life, but every life is remarkable, and worth studying. I had small opportunity for study of this. But I went across the road and joined the increasing assembly. He was lying in the middle of the small room into which the door opened. There was no fire on the broad hearth. "It's the first time that hearth has been cold for fifty years that I remember," said the landlord.

In the room were many evidences of the life he had led, memorials which no one now lived to cherish. An old musket and a muzzle-loading gun hung on one side of the room. The antlers of a moose and several of red deer were disposed as conveniences for hanging household utensils. Several strangely worn stones from rivers, curiously twisted and involved growths of trees, brilliant bits of mica and other minerals, were on the mantel-shelf over the fireplace. There was no ceiling to the room. The rafters were bare, and the sheathing on the sides was nearly black with smoke and time.

It was not the hour or place in which to indulge curiosity, but I could not shut my eyes to the surroundings out of which this life had gone. And when some one gave me a chair I found myself seated by a small solid table, on which lay one book, a copy of the Breeches Bible. It was verily a family Bible. It was an edition, if I remember aright, of 1595. And on the margins and blank reverses of leaves, in old and faded ink, there were pithy sentences written by generations of Scotch Presbyterians, of whom this man lying dead here was last. He, too, had gone to join the numerous company, among whom are martyrs and saints, and along his path, as he had travelled here almost a century, he had the same old guide-book they had used. It is a wonderful guide-book: good for men in the rush and crush of cities, as for men in the quiet, lonesome places of the up-country.

As he lay there men talked freely about him, and it was wonderful to hear the affection and respect which were universally expressed for him. Every one had loved him, and all alike felt the loss of a friend. On his farm, a hundred rods from the house, was a knoll which rose gently on one side some seventy or eighty feet, and from its summit fell off precipitously to the river which ran with loud voice over rocks below. It had been a favorite resting-place with the old man, and the young man when he was growing old. There were stones so arranged by accident that they made a seat, not very comfortable, but men do not seek cushioned resting-places in the up-country. He had seen suns rise and suns set many times, sitting there. Much of the gentleness of his nature had come from the long habit of sitting there a little while now and then and thinking. More had come from that old Bible; and the two—the holy book and the calm contemplation—had worked together in his soul. He had some favorite subjects of thought which he occasionally talked about. The marvel of the universe, which bothers philosophic theorists, was no marvel to him, but one grand fact which he realized. "I can never forget," said the village pastor, "how he impressed me with a sudden exclamation when we were talking about the discoveries of science and the laws of nature. He said, 'What idea can any man have of God who thinks, with his poor eyes and inventions of glass and brass, he can see into and across the whole province which his God governs.' Another time he said, 'I'm a Democrat with men, but with God there is no democracy, to my notion. Men get to preaching equality so much that they don't believe themselves any lower than the angels, and imagine that the universe is ruled by a Master who will exist or not, just as his subjects think best.'

"'Star-gazing you call it, do ye,' he said to one who saw him sitting on his porch one night. 'Yes, but I'm not looking at the stars; I'm looking between and beyond them, and I see a country out yonder in which there's no law of nature, no attraction, no force, nothing that I read about in men's books, only the will of God, which is light and force and law and all.'"

Such expressions indicate the effect on his mind of his habit of thought on the hill-top. In all times men have gone up into high places to think and to pray. There is no place so lonesome as the summit of a hill. It lifts a man out of the world. I have known many men, of utterly irreverent and thoughtless character of mind, awed and terrified at finding themselves on high mountain peaks, and afraid to stay there. I remember once, many years ago, when there was no hotel on Mount Washington, and I had gone up there intending to stay all night and see the sun rise, a sense of awe and lonesomeness overtook me which I vainly strove to resist. I had passed nights alone in forests, on the sea in an open boat, but this was intolerable. There was a feeling, indeed, of lonesomeness, but at the same time of being surrounded by an unseen crowd of witnesses. So I was driven down, and made my dangerous way into lower regions more associated with my young humanity.

But the old man was never alone on his hill-top, having in long years learned to talk much with the unseen who met him there, and look earnestly into space if perchance he might see there a vision of superhuman beauty. And one day he saw what he had waited for. It was a clear, cool summer day, with a north-west wind drifting clouds across an intensely blue sky. A neighbor who had occasion to see him, not finding him at home, walked out and up the hill just after sunset. The old man was sitting on the rock seat, reclining on another rock which supported his back and head. He had been looking into the depths of the clear atmosphere, and as he lay there looking, there came suddenly into his vision that which eye hath not seen from earthly mountain peak; ear hath not heard from voice, howsoever eloquent and musical; heart of man, even his gentle, thoughtful heart, had not conceived. Who shall attempt to say with what serene and solemn joy the old man had seen the blue heavens opened, and the glory that is not of sun or stars, and had entered into it!

VIII

OVER THE HIGHLANDS OF WESTERN NEW HAMPSHIRE

It was a fresh autumn morning when we left the village of New London, high up on the hills of central New Hampshire, and drove westward, without any definite idea of our destination.

New Hampshire possesses all kinds of scenery and soil. The northern mountain country falls off into a valley which crosses the western half of the State, in no very direct line, from the valley of the Connecticut near Hanover to the valley of the Merrimac near Franklin Falls. South of this valley—the west half of the State—running north and south, is a range of highlands, mostly now or formerly under cultivation, rising in farm-lands at times to a height which I believe is considerably more than 1000 feet above the sea. You know Mount Kearsarge, near North Conway. But few persons seem to know that there is another Mount Kearsarge in the State. This lies at the northern or north-eastern end of the range of highlands of which I speak, and is, in part, in the town of New London, or directly east of it in the next town. It is a very noble hill, rising alone out of the cultivated rolling lands. Away down in the south-western part of the State a similar mountain rises in stately grandeur, Monadnock by name, and thence the highlands of New Hampshire fall off gently towards Massachusetts.

This topographical account is not interesting, but it is necessary to understand it if you would understand carriage travel to the southward in the State, west of the Merrimac River. You can drive from the Profile House or the Crawford House to Hartford, following the valleys of the Amonoosuck and the Connecticut, without a hill of any account on the road. The scenery along the entire route is lovely beyond all praise, its variety infinite, its beauty equal in spring, summer, and autumn. The roads are, however, somewhat sandy and heavy, especially in dry weather.

You can also drive from either notch, Franconia or the Crawford, through the eastern part of New Hampshire southward to Massachusetts, over roads without severe hills and with varying scenery, most of it very beautiful.

But I prefer the hill roads through the highland country between the Merrimac and the Connecticut. These roads are in general good, the road-beds hard, and the many fine views repay the labor of climbing hills. Withal, horses do better, if carefully driven, on rolling than on level roads.

I had come from the Profile House down the Pemigewasset Valley through Plymouth to Bristol, thence across to New London, *via* Danbury, Wilmot, and Scytheville. At this last place I had reached the bottom of the cross-valley which I have mentioned, and thence the road to New London was uphill all the way, with Kearsarge on the left and behind us. New London is one of the high hill-towns, and every house in the village looks off many miles over fields and forests.

Turning the horses' heads to the southward, I could have gone down through Sutton and Bradford, and thence over tremendous hills to Washington. Turning them to the west, I should have a short drive to Lake Sunapee, which lies on the upland, surrounded by low wooded hills. I had driven both roads repeatedly. I am never tired of driving the last named, for it is exceedingly beautiful, and we chose it now.

In half an hour we were going through the dense woods which skirt Little Sunapee, the upper of a chain of three lakes, and of which you see only glimpses as you pass along by it, until you reach its outlet, which goes down into Otter Pond. Here the road strikes the upper end of Otter Pond, and sweeps around on its open shore for a quarter-mile. The pond is charming, a mile or two long and nearly as wide. The shore is clean sand and the water pellucid. I have waded off on this hard, sandy bottom and taken black bass with the fly, casting out to right and left, while my horses stood waiting on the road.

Fish Commissioners in some of our States have laboriously spoiled the fishing in a great many waters by introducing these black bass. Pickerel or perch or pumpkin-seeds are a more valuable food-fish to the farming population than black bass, and black bass when placed in a pond will destroy all other fish. It is only a question of time, and the destruction is sure to be complete, except in large bodies of water. The bass are protected by law till June 15th, and in some States till July 1st. In July and August they can be taken only with proper tackle and strong tackle, such as the farmer's boy does not possess. As soon as the weather and the water begin to grow cold, these fish begin to find places where they hibernate. After the middle of September they cannot be taken at all by any one with any tackle except in large lakes, and in those not after October. Here, then, is a fish of very small value to a population. It is time that all laws protecting them in the spring were repealed. Let the farmer get them whenever he can. There is no danger of their extermination—I wish there were; but if their increase can be kept down in the smaller lakes and ponds, it may happen that some other fish will survive.

We drove slowly around the head of Otter Pond,

then through the forest road along its rocky shore, with the water lapsing over the stones and making pleasant music in the sunshine. Then we came out of the woods at the little village of George's Mills. Here is the outlet of the pond, which falls over two or three saw-mill dams in its short course into Lake Sunapee. Sunapee is a large, wandering lake, presenting wherever you strike it abundant beauty of scenery. Bold, rocky headlands, covered with timber, jut out into it, and deep shadowy bays lie between them. I never yet have gotten to knowing which way is up and which way is down the lake or how it stretches its chief length. Properly speaking, this principal inlet, the only one of any account at George's Mills, ought to mark the head of the lake; but a long, narrow arm which goes far away to the eastward, along whose shores are villas and cottages, and which heads at Newbury, on the Concord and Claremont Railroad, always tempts me to consider that the upper end of the lake. However, there is no mistaking the outlet at Sunapee Harbor, into which I drove before dinner. Here Sugar River, a roaring torrent (depending on how high they lift the gate-way of the dam which holds back the lake), plunges down a steep declivity and finds the valley, through which it winds with clear and swift flow to Newport, and thence to Claremont and the Connecticut.

We dined, and then decided to linger for the day.

I took a boat and rowed miles and miles along the shores; landed here and there in golden forests or dark pine groves; cast flies where bass, if not yet gone to their winter sleep, ought to be found; took several that were not eight inches long, and were put back to go to bed and grow next year; and so idled away the afternoon. The night came on cold.

Next day we rode with the carriage-cover thrown back, to give us what warmth we might get from the sun shining through the still dense smoke. The road follows the river down to Newport; but we did not stop in that thriving town, except to post letters and send some telegrams. Driving through it, we crossed the valley and took the hill road to Unity or Unitoga Springs. This is a lonesome but very charming country-place, where are mineral springs and an old hotel. We had the house to ourselves; and again the loveliness of the atmosphere, the rich foliage on the near hills, and the dust of gold smoke that made a canopy over us and hid the far views, all tempted us to stay. I spent the afternoon in the woods on the shore of a small lake a mile from the hotel. I went there to fish; but the only boats on the lake were full of water, and there was no spot on shore where I could get out a cast of more than twenty feet. At that I took some perch and small pickerel with the fly, but gave it up soon and wandered in the woods, rich in ferns and mosses.

The next morning I sought and found a road,

before unknown to me, by which to reach the Connecticut Valley; for it was Saturday, and I proposed that my horses and I should rest over Sunday in the fine old village of Charlestown. It was only nineteen miles from Unity Springs, but in carriage travel we never, unless from some peculiar pressure, seek to accomplish great distances. The purpose is the enjoyment of the passing hours. I often linger along the road and cover only two or three or a half-dozen miles in a forenoon. So it was along this charming road. When I reached Charlestown I had driven only 108 miles from the Profile House in six days. Sometimes I drive 180 in the same time, taking the road leisurely and keeping the horses unwearied. I have known of gentlemen making 230 and 250 miles between Sunday and Sunday, with travelling carriages. But I have not known an instance of that kind which was not followed by the sickness of one or more of the horses that did it. The traveller by carriage must keep in mind that he is dependent on the good condition of his horses for continuous journeying, and must therefore care for them with unfailing watchfulness. It is more important that they should find a good stable than that he should find a good inn at night. He can put up with poor lodgings and food, and feel none the worse for it, whereas the dumb horse must suffer in a cold draughty stable, and may come out of it to sicken and fail along the road.

IX

THE TRIUMPHANT CHARIOT

THE rector told me the story as we stood in front of the church after morning service.

The church was almost hidden in a grove of maple-trees. It stood on the brow of a hill which overlooked one of the most lovely valleys on the sides of the Green Mountains. The road ran along the curve of the hill, in front of the church. The projection on which the church stood commanded a view both up and down as well as across the valley, which lay two or three hundred feet below. The mountain sloped upward, mostly forest-covered, behind the church. Across the valley was a similar mountain. The pasture lots went up, here and there, almost to the summit ridges. The head of the valley was only a half-mile above. Down from a ravine came a noble stream of water, and before it fairly reached the sloping valley-land it received two similar streams, the three alike falling over rocky beds with much noise and white confusion of waters before they came together into the comparatively peaceful river which flowed down through rich meadow-lands and away oceanward. For howsoever wild and vexed and unrestrained be the youthful flow of these our mountain streams, one and all alike are sure in time to reach the deep and solemn rest of the great sea.

Search the world over and you will find no landscape scenery to surpass these valleys which open away eastward and westward from the Green Mountains. The one we were in was like many others I had seen that spring, only these three grand cascades at the head gave it an individuality of its own.

On the lowland near the junction of the streams were a substantial stone house and a group of large and comfortable-looking barns and smaller buildings. This was the old home of a man whom the clergyman described as a noble specimen of that humanity of which, in country as in city, noble specimens are rare enough to be conspicuous.

"He feared God, but feared no man," was the summing-up sentence of the description. He was a man of wide influence, honored, respected, and loved, to whom for a half-century the old, and the young, too, had gone confidently for advice and help in joy and in trouble. For men and women need advice as often in one as in the other. It sometimes happens, in a community like this, that one man holds a commanding position. If he holds it steadily for a long time, so that he becomes the trusted counsellor and confidential friend of his neighbors, of all kinds, rich and poor, it is always certain that that man's life is governed by devout Christian principle. Others may be envied, imitated; others may win respect and admiration; but to become the confidential counsellor of all classes and ages, to be trusted with the troubles and invited into the happinesses of one's neighbors, it is essential to be loved as well as admired. And to be loved by all one must love all, not the good only, but the bad as well. And there never was, and never will be, a man who can love all classes of his neighbors and win their love in return, except that man have taken God for his example, whose spirit he has to some extent made part of his own. Reason, philosophy, experience, all affirm this. The idea that purity and peace, gentleness and affection, belong to what is called the religion of humanity, is disproved in the history of every nation, every city, every village and country community, among all peoples, civilized or savage, ancient or modern.

There is no more exalted position among men than that which was held by this man, growing old among the people who loved and respected him, doing good and getting good in every year of his long life. The world in which he lived was small, but it was large enough to occupy the energies of any mind, however able. The patriarchal system has never been improved on by organizing men into nations. One man in a country town can be worth as much to his age and to future ages, working at home, as he could be in a statesman's chair. This man had been the friend and counsellor of statesmen. No one can measure the extent of his influence for good. Its limit was not geographical, for it extended far beyond the boundaries of this small globe.

Much the clergyman told me of the personal and direct influence his old parishioner had exerted in the town, county, and State. But mostly he dwelt on the extreme beauty of his personal character and life, the delight with which the young people met him, his great grace of manner and voice, his devout and always cheerful bearing, his love of nature, his keen insight into character, his marvellous breadth of information and reading; and lastly, for all else was prefatory to this, he told me of the picturesque death of his old parishioner, counsellor, father, and friend.

All Friday and Saturday a north-east storm had raged among the hills; but Sunday morning the clouds went away before a stiff westerly breeze and the sun poured gold into the valley. The church was far away from any house—one of the old sites chosen in early days for people to come to from various valleys and hill-sides.

The man who had charge of the church had made a fire early in the morning before he recognized the fact that the cold storm was over. Heavy mists had rushed through the maples until nine or ten o'clock, and then the warm fresh, May air took their place. The interior of the church was not pleasant. The air was close. Perhaps for the first time in his eighty years of living, the Squire (as he was called, though he had never held an office) became sensible of physical suffering. So at least they supposed who saw him several times lift his hand to his head, and at length go to the side door and open it a little way and sit down near it. After a while, to the surprise of all, he noiselessly slipped out of the door and did not come back.

And now for the rest of the clergyman's story you will have to depend on imagination, or what we may intelligently believe who know and share the faith of the old man; for there was no one outside of the church to see him until all the people came out and saw him.

He sought the fresh air of the May morning. There was not enough of it among the maples; and perhaps he sought the sunshine with it. So he walked out of the grove towards the road-side, where his son-in-law, coming late and after the sheds were all occupied, had left his low carriage standing while he unhitched the traces and tied the horses in the grove. The empty carriage faced the south; it was on the open green, and sitting in it one could see a vast prospect up and down and across the valley. The sun shone in it and the wind blew over it. The old man took a seat in it, and before him lay the country in which he had lived and been loved, and far away yonder down the valley was a range of blue hills, beyond which was all the world and all the universe.

Thus far all this was a very simple and commonplace incident. Yes, but what seems the simple and commonplace may, by reason of what shall come next, be in reality the unintelligible and sublime. The old man had always lived close to another world. Many very dear ones had gone to it, and he had never ceased to regard them as living near him, nearer than if they lived in the flesh beyond those blue mountains. He never thought of doubting the reality of their life. He never argued about it, for his faith was above reason. Out of the church came the sound of the people's voices singing, and to him it seemed as if the people who were under the grass behind the church as well as they who were in the church were together praising God; for he was, whether he knew it or not, very near if not indeed on the ground where one may hear the voices of both worlds. So he leaned back and looked off and listened, and the wind played with his white hair; for he had left his hat in the church and sat bareheaded in the breeze and sunshine. Around him and above and in the valley and across on the other mountain-side began to gather appearances, if they were not realities. And who can say they were not realities? The white mists that were passing here and there among the trees near the summits, the snowy cataracts descending and shouting as they descended— were they water-falls and mountain-mists, or were they white garments? To your eye or mine they were the remains of last night's gloom and tempest; but what were they to his eyes, looking now through all things which stop our vision into the fathomless depths which lie beyond? To you or to me that tumultuous roar of the torrent was only the sound of many waters, the roar of streams filled full with heavy rains. So, perhaps, it was to him when he came out and climbed feebly into the carriage; but after a little there is small doubt that he heard the sounds of other waters falling from other hills into other valleys, the rivers with whose cadences our rivers keep some though faint and stammering harmonies. For all voices of winds and water-falls on earth—howsoever profane be the voices of men —all musical and melodious sounds of nature are part of the eternal song, and we should recognize it if we understood that music, as, perhaps, some time we may. Doubtless he heard, and though yet a man old and very feeble, began to understand the language in which the universe sounds its joy and praise. For the bright look that rested on his human face bore witness that before it became mere dead dust it had heard the sounds and seen the forms of another world. How long he sat there and looked and listened from the hill-side no one knows. Perhaps it was to the close of the service in the church. And when he heard the sound of the organ, and the voices of the people singing "Holy, holy, holy," the voices of the wind in the trees, and the voices of the waters thundering down the mountain, and the voices of the innumerable host whom we never hear except when, like him, we come to the entrance of the other existence, all together sounded through earth and heaven, and he heard them all; and hearing, joined in the anthem with them.

When the people came out of church they saw him sitting on the back seat of the carriage, his white hair fluttering in the wind, his hands folded on his lap, his eyes apparently looking across the valley at the opposite hill-side. A half-dozen people went to ask him if he was sick. They found him quite well; better than he had ever been. It was not a triumphal car, nor a chariot of fire; but he had gotten into it to go a short journey, and had gone, safely, happily.

X

A DEAD LETTER

ONE evening in May, many years ago, a man of an uncertain age, forty or fifty years old, perhaps, walked with a steady purposeful stride on this long road which leads winding through the primeval forests up the valley to a little settlement by a lake among the mountains. He carried nothing. He was a stranger. As now and then he passed a house the people wondered, and asked one another who he was. He reached the old church which stood at a crossing of the roads, the one going on up the valley, the other leading to right and to left over the hills. The minister's house was on the corner opposite to the church. The minister, a man in the prime of life, stood on the green in front of the church, looking over the stone-wall into the graveyard. He was thinking how many joys and pains, virtues and sins, were hidden there. He turned and saw the stranger striding towards him, and greeted him with a pleasant "Good-evening." The reply was not gruff, but short in tone, "Good-evening," and the man walked on; but his eye caught the horse-sheds in the rear of the church, and he stopped short, then sat down on the door-step.

The minister strolled towards him and asked him if he was going to the village. "Not to-night," was the curt, trisyllabic answer. The minister was a man of much experience. He saw that there was here something out of the common run of humanity in that neighborhood. "If you are not going farther you will want a night's shelter, unless you are going back again."

"I s'pose there's no objection to my sleepin' in one of them sheds."

"My house, over there, is more comfortable; come over with me and get your supper, and I'll give you a bed."

"I'm grateful for your offer, but I'd ruther sleep in the shed, and I don't need supper."

The minister urged his invitation, but could get no reply. The stranger sat silent, not even looking up or answering with his eyes. At last the minister gave him up and went home. He looked out in the twilight frequently, and saw the man sitting on the door-step. He went over and tried him again with pressure, but received no response. He somehow conceived the idea that the language used by the queer man was affected, and not natural; that he assumed to be what he was not, an uneducated man. Perhaps it was so, perhaps not; no one ever knew. For many years after that the stranger

lived in the valley, became one of the valley people, was known to every one, spoke to few, and used very brief sentences in such conversation as was necessary. He bought a tract of land, it could not be called a farm, lying on the side of the mountain and including a few acres of bottom land on the river. There were 100 acres in the tract, and he paid cash in bank notes, $80, for it. When the deed was made out, the village justice, who was a land-agent, asked him his name. He gave it promptly—Ben Layton. He built a log-house on his land. The people, not an æsthetic community, laughed at his selection of a site. It was up the mountain-side, on a projecting knoll, the front of which was a rocky precipice. The cabin stood in the edge of the forest. In front of it the ridge of the knoll was covered with low brush, mostly huckleberry bushes. A mountain stream came down a ravine behind the cabin and descended swiftly at one side of the knoll. A rough pathway, in time worn by his use, led from the cabin across the brook and down by the watercourse to the few acres of meadow-land on the river bottom. A forest road, little else than a logging road, among rocks and stumps, went from the meadow down two miles to the main road up the valley. From below you could see the cliff, and the low bushes covering the ridge, and the dark forest from which it projected, but you could not see the little cabin which stood under the trees. From the cabin door the view was one of unsurpassed beauty. The valley beneath, widening to hold a lovely lake two miles long, closing again where the mill and the store and the post-office and the half-dozen houses formed "the village," widened again beyond to the level where the church stood, and then went downward into immeasurable distance. The door opened to the west. When the sun was setting in June and July it went down in that remote distance, and the glory that filled the valley was like the light coming earthward from the celestial city.

Years went on. At first there was much curiosity about this strange arrival; but it passed. He became a recognized inhabitant. His strange character was more a matter of imagination than of known fact; for he seldom spoke to any one, and in those brief sentences which were necessary to his procuring the means of life he spoke as sensibly as any man in the valley. Oddly enough, he would sometimes exchange some little talk about the weather, or his health, or other commonplace subject, with the minister, but with no one else. And the minister was the only man who ever went twice to the cabin on the cliff. He had a settled conviction that this man had a soul, not disturbed by any errancy of faculty, which was worth looking after. And he looked after it for thirty or more years, but confessed in the end that he had never found it.

To the people the cabin was simply "Ben's cabin," and as years went along and young people came to exist who had not been there when he arrived, a stranger, he became Old Ben, a harmless semi-lunatic, who raised potatoes on his bottom-land, killed and ate woodchucks and all kinds of beasts of the field and forest, fished a great deal, but mostly wandered around in the woods and along the streams, silent and thoughtless.

Was he without thought? Who knows? Somewhere in the world perhaps there was one, perhaps there were many, who could have told what Ben had to think about. No one in the valley knew. He never read a newspaper or a book, never went to a public gathering, never voted, never was seen at church. He grew old. The minister grew old. All the people were growing older, many very old, as is the custom in city and country with all our family of man.

It was six o'clock of a July evening. A group of a dozen or more men stood on the porch of the store wherein was the post-office. The semi-weekly mail had arrived, and this group was regular at that hour. The minister sat in his low buggy under the shadow of a great Balm of Gilead-tree. The doctor drove up in his buckboard and stopped by the side of the minister. This was the time when the group at the post-office exchanged the news of the neighborhood, which meant a section of country three miles down and five miles up the valley, and included scattered clearings on the hills. The doctor, when he happened to be there, answered questions about the sick, and the intelligence he gave was carried in various directions, radiating to outlying homes, where all were sincerely interested in it.

"Doctor," said a man whose home was three miles away, "I shouldn't wonder if somethin's the matter o' Old Ben. I ain't seen him now it's a week or more, and I ain't seen smoke coming out of his chimeney for two days."

"Why haven't you gone up to see him?"

"Wall, it's somethin' of a climb, and a long way around, and Ben don't like company, and I've been purty busy hoein' potatoes, and I thought o' goin' up to-morrow."

"You might better have gone up to-night instead of coming down here. Does any one know whether Ben has been down the valley lately?"

"I seen him, lemme see—it was Monday a week ago—he was fishin' on the big rock. Hain't any of you fellows seen him sence then?" While they were, one and another, saying "No" to this query, the postmaster came to the door with a letter in his hand.

"Here's a letter for Old Ben. What had I better do with it?" The people closed around the postmaster. Here was an incident. A letter to any one of them would have been a matter of general interest, but a letter to Old Ben was a startling fact.

"It's come at last," said one.

"Yes, it's come at last," said another and another.

"As long as I've been postmaster—and that's been how many years, boys?—as long as I can remember, Ben has come every Saturday and asked if there was a letter for him. Sometimes he came twice a week, sometimes every day for a while. There ought to be something important in it, and he hasn't been here now for more than a week. He's been waiting more than twenty years for that letter, and it's come at last."

This constant application of Old Ben for a letter, persistent, though vain, for months and years, was a known fact to all the people; but it had long been set down as only another indication of his lunacy. Before sunset pretty much every family in the valley was talking about it, and saying, "Old Ben's letter has come at last."

The letter passed from hand to hand; one and another wondered who had written it. The minister and the doctor were conversing and had not heard the postmaster's questions. But they were talking about Ben. When the postmaster repeated his inquiry, the minister said:

"Give me the letter. I will take it to him. I am going out to see him."

The sun was just above the far horizon when the minister reached the end of the narrow rocky road on the bottom-land, and tied his horse under a rude cow-shed near the bars of the pasture lot. It was a good half-mile from this point, by the wild path up the side of a brawling stream, through primeval forest, to the level of Ben's cabin. The minister knew his way. He had been at Ben's cabin not a few times. There was no house or cabin or habitation of man within many miles that he had not visited often. But he had never been here at this hour. The sun had gone. A mass of clouds hung across the valley from mountain to mountain, and all were aglow with crimson light. The country below the arch of fire was lit with a golden lustre which came flooding up the valley from the clear sky on the horizon. Above all was crimson, below all was gold. Turning his back to the miraculous view, the minister struck the cabin door with his knuckles two or three times and waited. A robin in a tree near by sang out boldly. A thrush poured forth a flood of melody, and another lower down the hill answered him. No sound came from within the cabin. The minister knocked again and waited. While he was waiting he heard a step, and turning saw the doctor coming along the path around the corner of the cabin. He was not surprised. They two were in the habit of meeting on such errands at all hours of the day and night.

They went into the cabin. It was only one room, eighteen or twenty feet long and fifteen wide. All of one end was occupied by the heap of rough stone which formed the chimney. Along the side was a low, broad bench, which did duty for a bed. There was little furniture, but everything in the room was clean and neat. In, or on, the bed lay the tall form of a man, motionless. As the two approached him he made no sign. His eyes were open.

"Is he dead?" asked the minister. The doctor laid his hand on the man's forehead, and answered:

"No, he is living yet; but," he added, after a little, "he is near the end."

The same thought was in the minds of the two who sat by the side of the bed: "Who is this man that lies here dying alone in the forest?" They had time to think, for the twilight passed into night, and dark night, with clouds and rising wind, and the trees began to utter strange sounds, but there was no sound from the lips of Old Ben. A whippoorwill suddenly called with his clear, rich voice from the peak of the cabin, and a dozen or more answered from the woods below. The sounds of nature are innumerable in the night-time in still weather, and when the wind blows the forest is filled with voices in a thousand tones. Some are syllabic utterances, shouts, calls, and answers; others, long notes of delight or of pain. It made the silence of the cabin most solemn and impressive to hear the turmoil and tumult in the outer world. And it was the more oppressive to the two watchers in that he who lay there dying held a secret on which the silence seemed to be placing a great black seal; for, to say truth, they had within the past thirty years asked each other countless times, "Who is Old Ben?" To the people not given to much thought the question had long since lost interest. To them, reading, scholarly men, it had continuous and increasing attraction as an unsolved problem. They asked it now, one of the other, with their eyes.

"He will never get his letter after all," said the doctor, in a low voice.

"What letter?" The words came from the lips of the motionless man. Then a sudden flash of light illumined his face. They bent over him. "What letter?" he said again. "Is there a letter for me?"

"Give it to him," said the doctor.

"Yes, Ben, I have a letter for you. It came by the mail to-night."

"Give it to me, quick, quick, dominie, for she said—she said—;" he tried to lift his hand, but failed. The light on his face became white, cold. After a while the light reappeared in his eyes. "The letter—she said—" he was murmuring rather than speaking, and they could hear no more, for the wind thundered and the trees wailed and sobbed and shrieked. For one instant his eyes seized and devoured the letter which the minister held in his hand, but he was powerless to take it; and a few moments later the end came, and he was dead.

Their work was done. They lit their lanterns and went out, leaving the mystery behind them. The forest was never so black as in the contrast with their lights. The brook was a torrent, for heavy showers had been passing over. Even now, as they went cautiously down the narrow footway, they paused several times to listen to the reverberation of heavy thunder, or to recover eyesight lost in the dazzling brilliance of lightning.

"He never got the letter after all," said the minister, as they reached the low cow-shed under which they had left their horses. "What shall we do with it?"

In that part of the country in those days there was small thought or knowledge of the laws of inheritance. The public administrator was unknown. The people buried Ben. When they brought him out of the cabin they left the door open. There was nothing in it which any one wanted to steal, and there was no one who had any interest in preserving it.

The minister carried the letter back to the postmaster. It lay a long time in his office, and again and again was brought out and handed around among the people. It was the central point of interest in that valley for months—a small folded bit of paper, concerning which every man and woman within five miles of the place of its deposit thought and talked and guessed and wondered. Then it went the way of dead letters.

XI

EPITAPHS AND NAMES

THE frequency and the various conditions of country graveyards form a feature of New England landscape scenery peculiar to this country. You never see anything like it in any other country. It is, of course, common enough in Europe to find the old church surrounded by the church-yard. But our graveyards are very much more frequent without than with churches, or any buildings, in them; and churches are far more numerous without than with graveyards near them.

Most of the country graveyards are lonesome and mournful-looking places, often far away from any houses, frequently showing no indications of care nor any footprints of visitors. In and near the large villages one finds very beautiful cemeteries, demonstrating the existence of reverence for the place of final rest. But the lonesome burial-places that I pass along the road are for the most part open fields, with waving grass and golden-rod, and often thickets of brush, but without trees. This must not, however, be taken as evidence of forgetfulness of the dead, or intentional neglect of their graves. It proceeds simply from the fact that no one has suggested to the people the idea of combining effort to make the graveyard a place of beauty as well as of repose. It is in fact part of that lack of education in love of beauty which prevails among laborious communities, with whom life is a very constant struggle, whose days are none too long for the earning of a livelihood. True, it needs but an instructor to teach such communities the utility and money value of beauty, and show how the labor of the farm may produce beauty with profit. Doubtless after some more generations the education will come.

Meantime these desolate-looking burial-places contain abundant evidence of the refinement of mind which characterizes the country population; the deep sentiment which in human history accompanies the highest civilization. For if you desire to find communities in the largest measure composed of true gentlemen and gentlewomen, you are not to seek them in cities, nor in that section of city population sometimes called "society," but among the hills, in the up-country, where lives have grown old and generations have succeeded generations, far removed from the ambitions, the rivalries, the passionate collisions of the cities. Here are very kindly hearts, rejoicing in one another's prosperities, sympathetic one with another's troubles.

Here slander finds no encouragement and gossip has no life. Here no one tells lies about another, man or woman, and when men or women sin, as alas! they sometimes do everywhere, others do not enjoy talking about it, but are sorry and silent.

Doubtless there are evil-minded people in the country. Their number is increasing as railways bring the population into closer contact with crowded communities. But there remain, here and there, isolated tracts of country in which a great deal of the old purity of life and whole-souled love of neighbors yet prevails. If you know what that means, what it was a few years ago all over the north country, you cannot look at one of these road-side graveyards without recalling the scene which has been visible here, as each one of these mounds was heaped up. Then all the people from miles around came to the funeral, and whether it were old man or boy, babe girl or matron, no king had ever more royal burial, for none was ever laid in vault or ground with more solemn, loving, lamenting attendance.

I have often copied and printed epitaphs from these graveyards, which however rude or uncouth in expression, are nevertheless honest epitaphs. There is no introduction of the rivalries of society into these cemeteries. Simple, unpretentious headstones are here, only intended as marks of the separate graves, and the inscriptions are in plain letters, affectionate memorials. It is often interesting to see how frequently in the same graveyard the same epitaph is repeated. When first put on a stone it has attracted the eye and pleased the mind, and one and another has adopted it as just the expression of his or her feeling, and so it has been used on stone after stone. It is not uncommon to find stones which may indicate either the lack of a stone-cutter in the country, or the poverty which forbade employing one. These are home-made stones, and in their rude simplicity they are very eloquent, since you can but picture to yourself the survivor, in a solitary home, working slowly and patiently to carve the gravestone of the lamented dead. Here is an example. I found it in a graveyard in the western part of the town of Putney in Vermont. Type will not reproduce the rudeness of the lettering, but will exhibit the patience of the unskilled fingers which cut the characters deep in red sandstone:

>   H E R E L I E
>   S T H E R E
>   M E N S O F
>   M O S E S K E
>   R R W H O D I E
>   D N O V E M B E R
>   T H E 5 I N 1813
>   A G E D 65

Aside from the indications of human emotion which these records furnish in ancient as in modern cemeteries, they contain many curiosities of literature.

Mistakes in spelling, which are frequent, are of course the fault of the stone-cutter. It certainly was his fault in the case of a stone in the noble cemetery at Charlestown, N. H., whereon the inscription was clearly not intended to suggest the penance to which in old times some were occasionally addicted. The epitaph ends thus:

"His wayes were wayes of pleasantness
And all his paths were pease."

There is a common old epitaph, found frequently in graveyards in England as well as in America, in one or another form. In that same graveyard at Putney I found it in this form:

"Behold my grave as you pass by
As you are liveing so once was I;
Death suddenly took hold on me
And so will be the case with thee."

In a graveyard by the road-side in Charlemont, Mass., I found a variation, the first lines being:

"Come all young people as you pass by,
As you are now so," etc.

In that Charlemont burial-place I copied from

the grave of Mr. Nathaniel Upton, who died in 1829, this short, sharp statement:

> "Here lies my friend
> Till time shall end."

Manchester in Vermont, one of the most beautiful villages in the world, has a cemetery which, like the village, may claim superior beauty to almost any other in the north country. Wandering through it, I copied this inscription from a stone marking the graves of three children, who died in the years 1821, 1823, and 1824:

> "Here in the dust 3 babes we
> Sleep by our Father here
>   our Mother Brothers
> Sisters dear have left us
>   alone to moulder
>   here"

And another, over a young wife, only eighteen years old, who died in 1810.

> "Mourn not for me
> Wipe off the crystal tear
> Your allotted portion be
> Like mine upon a bier.
> Go search the earth around
> Regard well your behaveer
> To Jesus Christ you're bound
> He is your only Saviour."

At Fayetteville in Vermont I strolled into the

old graveyard, and copied here and there an inscription.

On one stone I found this:

> "Now, little James has gone to rest
> With Eliza Ann among the blest.
> Aside by side their bodies lay.
> Till the great resurrection day."

On a stone by the side of the above:

> "Oh, little Lavina she has gone
> To James and Charles and Eliza Ann.
> Arm in arm they walk above,
> Singing the Redeemer's love."

On a somewhat large monument was a photograph, or perhaps it was a daguerreotype, set deep in the stone, and under it the familiar old epitaph before mentioned, with, however, a stanza added which I do not remember to have seen elsewhere:

> "Behold my friends as you pass by," etc.

> "What thou art reading o'er my bones
> I've often read on other stones,
> And others soon shall read of thee
> What thou art reading now of me."

There is a quaint force in this, which is from an 1825 stone at Pittsfield, N H.:

> "Ah soon we must persue
> This soul so lately fled
> And soon of you they may say too
> Ah such an one is dead."

And on another stone in the same yard I found this brief sentence:

"Death is a debt to nature due
I've paid the debt, and so must you."

Sometimes I find hints of tragedies or romances in the quiet up-country lives which have found final peace under the stones. As I drove by a little cemetery in Goshen, I stopped the horses and read from the carriage an inscription which has given me food for a thousand imaginings since. I wondered what could have been the story of that life which was thus published on the road-side, manifestly with intent that every passer-by should read. I even had the curiosity to inquire, but found no one who remembered the events alluded to. It was the grave of a girl of seventeen, and the epitaph was this:

"Dearly beloved while on earth—
Deeply lamented at death—
Borne down by two cruel oppressors—
Distracted and dead."

Peace be with the child, whoever she was and whatever her sorrow! It was a lonely graveyard, far away from any village, and not near any house, but there was a goodly company of the sleepers near her on the hill-side going up from the road, and she is not alone in her rest, and will not be alone in the morning.

Sometimes I have found very touching evidences of the grief that comes to all human hearts alike, in city and country, in Christian and pagan lands. There is an affectation of sorrow in some tombstone literature, but I don't think any one will imagine there was not the outburst of a mother's heart in the words that were on the tombstone of the child named Coral. She was but fourteen years in this country, and some one—it could have been but one—when she went suddenly away, summed up her agony in the words on the stone, "My dearest love, my dearest love!" In a city cemetery we do not fancy that the publication of one's private grief seems in good taste even on a memorial stone. But no one can find fault with any inscription which bears evidence that it is uttered, not to the living who remain, but to the dead loved one who has gone on. Such inscriptions properly dedicate memorial stones.

Some graveyards, full of the graves of the old-time folks, are abandoned as if forgotten. At Francestown, N. H., I found such a place. The stones were lying or leaning down in all directions. It was difficult to read the inscriptions. Brush and weeds concealed graves and stones. Here are some lines from the headstone of Mr. Isaac Brewster, who died in 1782:

> "Happy the company that's gone
> From cross to crown, from thrall to throne

How loud they sing upon the shore
To which they sailed in heart before."

Driving up the road from Keene, N. H., to Drewsville, I reached a little road-side inn in the town of Surry, at about the time to feed my horses. As I sat on the front steps of the inn, the scene, in the noon of a bright October day, was not exhilarating. There was no village. Across the broad road was a church. The front platform was rotted, and the broken plank, some standing on end, made it unnecessary to ask if it was abandoned. There was a graveyard a little way from it, a blacksmith's shop, and a building, half town-hall and half grocery-store, standing between. The graveyard, although apparently not in use, was evidently cared for. It was neat and in good order. Perhaps the church is deserted because the population is less. Whatever be the reason, I have rarely found a country graveyard which was better worth visiting.

There was a very large group of graves of one family, the name varying, usually Darte, sometimes Dort, sometimes Dart, and among them Eli, Elihu, and Eliphalet. One of the little girls was named Azubah. Mr. Nathaniel Darte died long ago at 66. There was a blank on the stone where the year of his death should have been. His headstone said:

"Dear friends don't mourn for me nor weep;
I am not dead, but here do sleep.

> And here I must and shall remain
> Till Christ does raise me up again."

Doubtless he was a resolute man, in death as in life. Mrs. Deborah Darte, his wife, died in 1773, only twenty-eight years old. She says:

> "Friends retire; prepared be
> When God shall call to follow me."

When Mrs. Darte died she left two little daughters, Avis and Eunice. This we know from their graves, close by. They both grew up. Avis married Asa Holmes, and in 1791, a young wife in her twenty-second year, "fell a victim to death." The errors in spelling on her tombstone must be charged to the stone-cutter of the day. This is the epitaph:

> "Altho' I sleep in death awhile,
> Beneath this barron sod,
> Ere long I hope to rise and smile,
> To meet my savour God."

Little Avis and Eunice grew to womanhood during the trying times of the Revolutionary War, but did not live to see the good times of this nineteenth century. For Eunice, who was only two years old when her mother died, Avis being four, died unmarried a few months after her sister in 1791, in her twentieth year. Mrs. Eunice the headstone calls her, that is, Mistress Eunice. I fancy she had received this title, given in those days to maiden ladies, but not often to those as young as she, because she had become the head of her surviving father's household. She was doubtless a fair New England maiden, lovely and loved. Was it a lover who called her "friend," in her epitaph? Or was it her father? For as we will see presently the word "friend" had endearing associations in that locality, and a father might apply it to a daughter or a husband to a wife, according to modern French usage. Here is her epitaph, literally:

> "Stop gentle youth and drop a tear,
> For my true friend lies buried here.
> She once was innocently gay,
> But now a lifeless lump of clay.
> Then pity my sad overthrow,
> Nor set your heart on things below."

When Ruel Mack died in 1812 he left this assurance, as we find it carved over him:

> "Mourn not for me, nor thus reflect,
> But all your sighs and tears suppress,
> Since God has promised to protect
> The widow and the fatherless."

Mr. Woolston Brockway, who died in 1789, in the seventy-eighth year of his age, was verily one of the New Hampshire fathers. The stone record says: "He left a widow and eighty-seven children, grand and great-grandchildren." Of John Brockway, who died in 1799, it is said:

> "He lived a friend to all mankind
> And died in hopeful peace of mind."

On the headstone of Mrs. Lucina Willcox, who died in 1800, is a version of a familiar old epitaph, before mentioned, whose peculiarity I italicize:

> "Death is a debt by nature due,
> *I've paid my shot* and so must you."

Theodosha, wife of Edmund Wetherbee, died in 1806 at twenty-one years of age, and her husband thus laments:

> "Why do I mourn beneath the cross?
> Why do I thus repine
> If God be pleased to take away
> A lovely friend of mine."

In 1802, when Benjamin Isham was laid in the ground, they carved this over him:

> "Pray don't lement when death is sent,
> Nor fill a watery eye;
> It was decreed to Adam's seed
> All that are born must die."

John Marvin went away triumphantly in 1807, a soldier of the church militant who fell in the battle. There is the ring of a clarion in his epitaph. If you do not think so, go and read it as I read it in a golden October day, with a north-west wind rushing over the hills and sweeping the yellow maple-leaves in wild and musical whirls around you in that otherwise silent burial-place, while above you is the blue sky into which so many have looked from these hills and valleys, and looking have gone to meet their leader:

> "Death, thou hast conquered me—
> I, by thy darts, am slain;
> But Christ has conquered thee,
> And I shall rise again."

I lingered two hours in this lonesome burial-place, copying quaint epitaphs: those of the Reverend Zebulon Streeter and Tabitha, his consort, who died in the early part of the century, of Abia Crain, of Colonel William Bond, of Simon Baxter, and a number more which are in my note-book. Let it suffice to add only that of Mr. John Redding, who died in 1814. It is very homely:

> "The widow mourns the loss of a husband near,
> The children of a parent dear;
> But still one comfort does remain,
> The hopes that our loss is his infinite gain."

As I was coming out of the ground I was startled at sight of a tall, white stone, and the legend, "Ichabod Crain died Oct. 14, 1866, æ. 82 years and 10 months." The spelling was not that of Geoffrey Crayon, but by the side of this stone was another, whereon I read: "Fanny, wife of Ichabod Crane, died March 22, 1842, æ. 53."

There is an interesting old cemetery at Norwich in Vermont, where I passed a rainy Sunday.

The stones of a hundred and more years ago are going rapidly to decay; many inscriptions are already lost past all recovery; parts of others are gone. I hope there is a local historical or other society which has preserved accurate copies of these old records. They will always be of inestimable value, not alone to descendants of those who lie here, but to local and general historians.

It was raining, and the yellow grass was high and wet; but I forgot the dismal weather as I went on from one to another old stone, and kneeling in the grass studied out, sometimes copying, the inscriptions. I found several names of women, uncommon though none entirely new to me, such as Mindwell, Thankful, Salla, Alba, Candace.

Here is an inscription from an old stone:

"In memory of Mr. Nathaniel Hatch who died with the small pox at Charlestown N. H. July 3, 1776 aged (blank) years. His bones were accidentally found in 1810 by men to work on a turnpike between Charlestown and Walpole and deposited at this place by the desire of his son Oliver Hatch of this town.
Let not the dead forgotten lie
Lest men forgit that they must die."

That stone speaks of the terror which accompanied the disease when it appeared at Number Four (the ancient name of Charlestown), the hasty, unmarked burial, not in the general graveyard. It may suggest, too, that Americans had many subjects of personal thought and work and worry on the 4th of July, 1776.

The small stone at the grave of Mariah Hatch, who died in 1802, after living five weeks, gave opportunity to some one to defy orthography and orthodoxy and the doctrine of original sin, in this epitaph:

> "Beneth a sleeping infant lies
> To earth her body's lent,
> More glorious she'll hereafter rise
> Though not more inocent."

The freedom of the country stone-cutter from all laws of calligraphy and orthography is exhibited in an inscription which I copy line for line:

> "In memory of Mrs Susannah
> wife of Ensign Elisha Burton
> who died in full assurance
> of a Beter life April 27 1775
> in ye 23d Year of her Age she
> was an Obliging wife a tender
> Mother & a Sincear Christion
> born From above she paied
> her viset here & then Retorned
> to Dwell with saints on high
> where she is Ceased From
> Every ancious Care & Joined ye
> Geniral Chorus of ye Joy"

Evidently the last word should have been "sky."

There is something worth your philosophic study in these graves, and in graves which you may find scattered all over the world, which you may classify as you classify birds and fish and mammals and flowers, placing them together. All these people died in one faith; all are of one family. It strikes me always as very odd, very unscientific, for men to neglect great moral facts, and great physical facts which seem to be consequences of moral facts. Thousands of people swarming together periodically towards central points, called places of worship, are as distinctly phenomena as any other physical occurrences in this world. The impelling causes, if natural, demand the highest attention of the philosopher. If they are not natural, then they are supernatural, and annihilate many of the speculations of the small philosophers of our day.

What higher philosophy is there? It is written, in ill-spelled phrases but in words of wonder, all over these rude stones in the up-country graveyards. "You can't read it," do you say? Come, and I will show it to you in plain letters of modern cutting. For as the rain fell steadily, and the clouds dragged down lower on the valley, and it grew colder and colder, I was about to come away from the old graveyard, when I saw the dense, dark mass of a low spruce bending its branches heavy with wet down to the ground. Parting the branches, I found a brown stone, surmounted by a cross, and read the summing up of that sublime faith which makes an old New England graveyard to be holy land. "O JESU QUI MIHI CRUCIFIXUS ES IN TE SPERAVI."

An interesting subject of thought is found in the Christian names which have been given to children, borne through longer or shorter lives, and finally carved on gravestones. Whence came some of these names, especially as names given to female children? Here are a few out of many which I have copied in various burial-places along the roads. Some are Scriptural, varied in spelling, some noteworthy only for the spelling:

Vesta,	Smilinda,	Bezaleed,
Madona,	Theodate,	Phileena,
Imagene,	Mitty,	Asenath,
Sabrisal,	Rozill,	Resolved,
Alanette,	Lima,	Comfort,
Rocksena,	Orlo,	Romanzo,
Ora,	Elmon,	Theda,
Phene,	Ede,	Diademia,
Arozina,	Irena,	Coral.

While on this subject of names of the dead, here is an illustration of names now in use by the living. In a village inn in New Hampshire I found the printed catalogue of a school located there, and copied in my note-book the following Christian names of young lady students:

Myrtie Ioline.   Mary Etta.
Una Gertrude.   Margaret Marilla.
Mary Adella.   Lora Eliza.
Lois Ella.   Franca Lydia.
Corrie Elbra.   Fannie Mae.
Daisy Sarah.   Minnie Etta.
Hattie Rose Pearl.   Lizzie Estelle.
Myrtie Kate.   Mary Loraine.
Florence Genevra.   Bernette Samantha.

Here is an interesting study. Doubtless in each family there was a satisfactory reason for the name given to the child, however strange the names appear when brought together in a catalogue. Frequently a mother desires to perpetuate in her daughter the name of the father, grandfather, or other male relative. In such cases names of men are slightly transformed to become feminine in sound. Several times I have been told by a mother that she had named her child from a character in a book which she had read, and that not liking the name as found, she had altered it a little. Often a young mother, full of joy and love, gives her baby the name of a flower. It is not often that parents, in naming children, take into thought the possible maturity and old age of the child, sent on in life with a label that cannot be well effaced. In a Vermont cemetery is the grave of a child who lived two years, till 1824, weighted with the name Orsamealius Almeron.

Turning over an English publication recently, I read a note concerning a person who died a long while ago. The writer, to verify his accuracy as to the date of the person's death, stated that his coffin-plate is preserved in the family residence. I do not know whether this indicates a custom to any extent prevalent in England, of preserving coffin-plates instead of burying them with the dead. It may be only an accidental preservation. But I am sure it is not generally known that such a custom has long prevailed in many parts of New England. In carriage travel I have frequently found the custom in practice. I once stopped for dinner at a farm-house and inn, in a village in Connecticut. We waited awhile in the little parlor, which was filled with family treasures in the way of curious and pretty things on shelves and pictures on the walls. Among the latter, framed separately under glass and hanging in different parts of the room, were three plain silver coffin-plates, engraved in the usual way with the names, ages, and dates of death of members of the family. This was the first instance in my experience of this custom, which, I learned, was common in the neighborhood. Afterwards I met with the same custom in various parts of other New England States, and it is quite likely that it prevails elsewhere in the country.

Opening a drawer in my library, I happened on some small wooden tablets which I found many years ago in Egypt. One of them, for example, is about four and a half inches long by three and a quarter inches wide. Notches are cut in the sides near one end, which is also perforated with a round hole. This was for a string. On one side of the tablet is carved in deep, rude letters, a Greek ininscription: Σαραποδερος Κτὶ Καλετος ετ' μ': "Sarapoderos Kti, son of Kales, aged 48."

The same words are written in ink on the other side of the wood. Here is the close counterpart, 1800 years ago, of the modern coffin plate. For these wooden tags were attached to the mummied bodies of the dead, as records to go with them to the burial.

Every work of art is as much an embodiment of thoughts as a written sentence or a book. To look at works of art and express opinions as to their merit or demerit, to criticise them, is trifling work of little value. To read works of art as historical and personal records is the business of the art student. Here is a remarkable series of works of art, made by men in remotely separated periods, which evidently spring from one and the same motive. While we say at once that here is an indication, slight but noteworthy, of the sameness of ancient and modern humanity, we are nevertheless somewhat in the dark as to this one common motive. What is it? We have similar, though not identical, works in gravestones and monumental inscriptions.

I do not speak of the marking by inscriptions of the resting-places of the dead. That is more easily accounted for. But why this custom of the ages, pagan and Christian, of placing with the dead the record of how many years he or she had lived?

In the vast numbers of ancient mortuary inscriptions which we possess, this record is of constant occurrence. AURELIA *dulcissima filia quæ de sæculo recessit vixit ann.* XV., M. IIII. ANTIMIO vixit annis LXX. JULIA PROCILLA vixit ann. XIX. Innumerable examples like these occur, especially in early Christian times. The phrase, "lived so many years," is the common, often the only, inscription accompanying the name. Often the length of the lifetime is stated even to months and days. Why this custom?

I do not attempt to answer the question. It is easy to find reasons for epitaphs in general. They are various, under various circumstances. Some, many, are importunate appeals to the living for sympathy in sorrow. Some are designed to perpetuate loved or honored memories. Not a few which speak passionate grief are but sounding phrases, published to deceive the people into believing in a sorrow which does not exist. Many are devised as sermons to the active world, and many are placed only in obedience to existing custom. But I cannot see clearly what has been the constant motive of survivors in burying their dead with the statement that he or she had lived so many years and months and days. Purposes of identification do not account for it satisfactorily.

Professor A. C. Merriam, in a monograph upon the Egyptian tags, says that of the small number known there are two classes, one class evidently used to direct transportation of the body from the place of death or of embalmment to that of entombment. He gives an example of this kind of tag, which reminds us of the address of a modern express package: "To Diospolis; Pamontis, son of Tapmontis; from Pandaroi." The other class, to which mine belong, went into the tomb attached to the body.

These little wooden tags are objects of no small interest. They are probably not older than the beginning of the Christian Era—perhaps belong to the second century. They speak a mystery, the mystery I have already indicated. Whatever the motive be of recording the age of the dead, it is certain that there has always been a prevalent idea among men which has led to the placing with the dead sometimes records, sometimes personal objects. In countless cases we know that this idea has been an avowed belief in the immortality of the soul, and the added faith in a resurrection. Has a like faith, sometimes so faint as to be unconfessed, led to the custom in all cases? Did those who buried the son of Kales follow him in vague imagination to the world of spirit, and thus, almost unconsciously, regard his life as continuous, unbroken, while they thought of this life in the body as only a section off from the beginning of the endless continuity? Is there in all these inscriptions an eloquence which those who made them did not clearly recognize; which would be made plain by adding the word "here?"—"Julia Procilla lived here nineteen years." If that were the inscription, or if that be the sense in which it was carved, then it ceases to be a mere statement of fact, and rises to the highest rank as a simple and powerful epitaph. And it is quite probable that on Christian graves this is the true intent in the use of the word *vixit*—lived.

Was Sarapoderos one of the Christians of the Church of St. Mark? Was this tablet-tag intended to tell the Arab of later ages who should rob his grave, and me and all others to whom the inscription should come, that he passed the first forty-eight years of his existence here, in what men call "living," and then went to the other living, where he now is and will be forever?

That common epitaph:

> "As you are now, so once was I,
> As I am now so you must be—"

brought to mind an ancient inscription said to be found on a Roman tablet at Naples, "*Fui non sum: estis non eritis: nemo immortalis.*"

The similarity and the immeasurable difference between the two epitaphs is manifest The philosophy is in comparing the human minds, 2000 years apart, which inscribed them on the tomb of the dead. In both the idea is a message, a voice, from the dead to the living. In both is the sad ring of human consciousness of brief existence, universal certainty of the close of this life. But while the ancient ended his words with the profoundly gloomy "no one is immortal," the modern closed his with the assurance of another life and the words "follow me."

In no custom of men is there more evidence of the community of mind, the sameness of qualities in the soul, than in the custom of placing epitaphs over the dead. Nor can we, I think, find in any literature more interesting illustration of the identity of the race in all ages.

There are ancient epitaphs which are identical in sentiment with hundreds to be found in New England and Old England graveyards. My notes contain many such. It is common enough in our time for parents to record in stone their grief, as if demanding sympathy in their affliction from even strangers, and the passers-by of future times. "My darling, my darling," were four words which I copied from a child's gravestone one day; "Our dear little one," from another; scores of like expressions you are familiar with. How like the sentiment to that of ancient parents. At Aquileia, ages ago, Aurelius and Prima, father and mother, made a tomb for their little Aurelia, named doubtless for her father, and wrote on it *"Aureliæ, animæ dulcissimæ: quæ vixit in pace ann. IIII. men. VI. diebus XXIII."*

They loved that "sweetest soul." "She lived in peace," for they had made home peaceful, and she had brought peace with her in the household. They counted in memory every short year of the four, every moon of the six, and they treasured with devout love each hour of the twenty-three days which were last in the short life of their joy. Many a modern father and mother have knowledge of the emotion which led them to carve this epitaph.

And that custom of recording even the days of a beloved life, ancient and modern, on innumerable stones, reminds me, in passing, of an inscription at Rome which went still further, thus : *"Vix. Ann. XIX., M. II., D. IX.: horas scit nemo"*—"She lived nineteen years, two months, nine days, hours no one knoweth."

Not alone parents to children, but husbands and wives to one another, and children to parents, placed in ancient as in modern times, memorials of affection and respect, carved on stone for perpetuation. At Naples Proculus and Procillanus made a monument to Marcia, *"Matri Sanctissimæ"*—"their most holy mother." Somewhere, I forget where, a Roman husband said of his wife, on her gravestone, "*Nil unquam peccavit, nisi quod mortua est*"—"She never did a wrong, except that she died."

It is very rare indeed to find on a modern tombstone a doubt of immortality. Once I copied an epitaph in which occurred the distinct assertion that the man who lay there believed in no God. Whether he ordered the record, or another placed it there without direction, I know not. I have a note of a Roman epitaph, "*Vixi et ultra vitam nihil credidi*"—"I have lived, and I believed in nothing beyond this life." Another of two "most sad" parents over a loved child expressed despairing grief in terms of bitterness: "We are cheated in our votive offerings; we are deceived by time, and death laughs at all our carefulness: Anxious life comes to nothing."

XII

FINDING NEW COUNTRY

LEAVING Franconia one may drive north or south, as he pleases, until well away from the high mountains, and then take such direction as may tempt him. A magnificent drive is through Bethlehem, Whitefield, Groveton, North Stratford, to Colebrook, which is on the upper Connecticut River; thence eastward across the State through Dixville Notch to Errol on the Androscoggin; thence along the west side of Lake Umbagog to Upton, and down the Bear River Notch to Bethel in Maine. This drive, easily accomplished in a week, is full of delights. It is in large part through wild country, but the roads are in general better than in the more southern country.

Southward from the Profile House the road follows the Pemigewasset River and valley to Plymouth, some thirty miles. The traveller going towards home in Massachusetts or elsewhere in the lower country, may follow the river road to Bristol and Franklin Falls, and then go down the bank of the Merrimac through Concord. Or he

ON THE PROFILE ROAD

may take a route through the middle of the State, over highland country, or he may cross the State to the Connecticut valley, and go southward along that river.

If in leaving the mountain country he desires to go nowhere in particular, only to wander along the roads, he can do no better than to drive into northern Vermont. The direct route from Franconia is through Littleton, and, crossing the Connecticut at Waterford, to St. Johnsbury.

By way of finding new country, I drove from Franconia to Lancaster in New Hampshire.

From Lancaster we drove across the Connecticut into Vermont, and down the river. We did not start until afternoon, thinking not to go beyond Lunenberg Heights. That little village stands on a hill, with a grand view of the Franconia and White Mountain ranges, the valley of the Connecticut lying some four or six hundred feet below, in the foreground of the landscape. The air was smoky, and we could not get all the extent of this grand outlook. As the afternoon was not far advanced, I decided to go on westward.

If you will look at a map you will see that Lunenberg lies about forty miles south of the Canada line, and due east of St. Johnsbury. Going northward in Vermont you can follow up the valley of the Connecticut to the Canada line by a road along the river, or you can follow up the valley of the Passumpsic River, from St. Johnsbury, and diverging at West Burke, go north along the eastern side of Mount Annanance (on Lake Willoughby) to Island Pond, and thence on to Canada. Between these two routes there is no northward route through this north-eastern part of Vermont. Nor is there any practicable road from east to west across any part of this section. The road I was driving that afternoon, from Lancaster to St. Johnsbury, is the most northern road in Vermont, going west from the Connecticut River, across this part of the State. There was a poor road once along the track of the Grand Trunk rail from North Stratford to Island Pond, but it has not been kept up as a summer road, and is not safe. There is a mountain road across from Guildhall to Burke, but it is so rough that only necessity should lead any one over it with a light wagon. I have only to add that I do not recommend this road from Lunenberg to St. Johnsbury.

Two miles out from Lunenberg the road became narrow, and deep mud holes and deeper dry holes were frequent. Then it became rough and rocky. This is not an untravelled road. It is in constant use. We met fifteen vehicles—heavy farm wagons, covered buggies, and others—and the meeting in narrow passes, among rocks or mud holes, was serious business. I suppose the condition of this road is due to the system of road-making by town tax. Lunenberg is not a rich town, is sparsely settled, and this road, the most northerly cross-road from St. Johnsbury to the Connecticut, is used more by non-residents than residents. It presents a strong argument for a new system of public roads used by the public. When the States utilize State prison and county jail labor on road-making they will have better roads, no dispute with labor societies about prison labor, increase the taxable value of farm property, and add to the intelligence and home-loving character of the population, as well as add to the population. Railroads have cursed and depopulated Northern New England. Good wagon roads are needed for the restoration of the country. What is true of this part of the country is true in many other States of the Union.

Three hours of the golden afternoon it took me to accomplish five miles. Then we entered the town of Concord. But the sun was setting, and St. Johnsbury was yet sixteen miles away. If the road were to be of the same sort we should hardly get through at all in the dark; so we began to think of a stopping-place. Two miles on we drove into a little saw-mill village at the outlet of Miles Pond, famous for pickerel, and we were told that there was no inn in the village, but that travellers were sometimes "accommodated" at the house of a hospitable family, to which I drove. It was the last house in the village, a small, unpainted, one-story house, on the bank of the pond, and the tired horses gladly stopped on the grass before the door. A lady was sitting on the stoop, sewing by the last of the daylight. Could they take care of us for the night? She could not say; her husband would be at home from the field very soon; she could take care of us, but he would have to say whether he could take care of the horses. We must await his coming. So we threw blankets over the horses and waited. The twilight came down. My rod, as always, was lying in the carriage, and I put on a large white fly and went to the shore of the pond. Two or three casts to get out line, then a long back cast, and—my fly was on a telegraph-wire which was high overhead behind me—and the leader went into a mass of raspberry-bushes along the bank which overhung the water. Telegraph-lines are among the abominations of anglers. They penetrate the wildest woods, and arrest one's cast in the most unexpected places. I have left flies on telegraph-wires all over the world. No amount of experience serves to make one careful. Three successive casts I left on a wire between Saltzburg and Ischl. Now I put on another fly, and threw it out among the stars, which were plenty and silvery in the calm depths under the lily-pads. No pickerel should have been out so late, but there was one half-pound fellow who was still abroad, and he took the fly; and while I was landing him our host arrived, and said he could take care of the horses. So we went in, and were most kindly and hospitably treated. The little house held us comfortably. We had a broiled bird, eggs on toast, and abundant doughnuts, and cakes of various kinds, and milk in plenty for supper.

The road was good next day through West Concord to St. Johnsbury, where we dined, and that evening we rested at Danville Green.

Danville Green will assuredly be better known in future years. It is a little village on a lofty piece of upland farming country, commanding a majestic view. The most striking feature in this view is the eastern horizon, which is formed by the New Hampshire and Franconia mountains. Of these there is scarcely a known peak which, seen from this angle, is not brought out separately against the sky. Thus the White Mountain or Presidential Range, from Madison and Adams to the Crawford Notch, and the Franconia Range from the Crawford Notch to Lafayette and Kinsman, are laid out in a succession of elevations, while Moosilauke, at the extreme right, ends the serrated horizon line.

Joe's Pond lies a mile or two to the westward of Danville Green, and Molly's Pond a few miles farther to the west, on the road we drove towards Montpelier. The waters of the former flow into the Connecticut, while the latter pours out in a fine stream which is one of the heads of the Winooski, or Onion River, emptying into Lake Champlain.

On this outlet of Mollie's Pond is one of the finest cascades in the country. The stream, which has been rushing and roaring along its rocky bed, suddenly plunges down the hill into the valley in a white torrent. The fall may be 150 feet in height, not perpendicular, but over a series of steep, rocky steps. The forest overhangs it on both sides. If you are driving down the valley from Cabot your road passes directly in front of this magnificent water-fall. Were it in Switzerland it would have wide renown. On the direct road leading from Danville to Marshfield the cascade is not visible, though its roar comes out of the forest on your right as you pass near it. The cascade is known hereabouts as Molly's Falls. Molly's Falls are on Molly's Brook, and Molly's Brook flows from Molly's Pond.

Joe and Molly are historical characters in the Coos country. Joe was a young Indian from Nova Scotia who, on the practical destruction of his tribe after the siege of Louisburg, drifted to the St. Francois tribe, and made his home on the Connecticut where Newbury now is. He was always on kind terms with the early settlers, and lived to a good old age, enjoying a pension from Vermont until his death in 1819. In his early days he took a wife (known to the whites as Molly) who had by a former husband two sons named Toomalek and Muxawuxal. The latter died. The former lived to be a grief to his mother. He is described as a short, broad, fiendish-looking, bad Indian. He desired for his wife a young girl, Lewa, who preferred and married another. Whereupon Toomalek, watching for his opportunity to kill the favored lover, now the husband, saw the two sitting by their camp-fire in the evening, shot at the man and killed the wife. The Indians tried him by their law. Old chief John, a renowed warrior, presided, and laid down the law that as Toomalek had shot at the husband and missed him, he had committed no crime as against him; that as he had not intended to shoot the woman in shooting at the man, the occurrence was accidental so far as she was concerned. So they discharged him. But John lived to repent his small knowledge of the distinct crimes of murder and manslaughter. Toomalek shortly after killed the husband in a fray, and again went free, it being adjudged that he acted in self-defence. It was old John who saved him again by his legal acumen.

Old John's eldest and favorite son, Pial, with other young Indians, was walking across the fields now in North Haverhill, when an exchange of words sprang up between him and an Indian girl. She whispered in Toomalek's ear, and he, turning short, drove his knife through Pial, then and there killing him, contrary to Indian and white law and the peace of both communities. This time the whites undertook to administer justice, and they did it with a queer intermingling of white and copper-colored law and practice. The court was apparently a town meeting, called at Newbury the morning after the murder, and the judgment of death was unanimous, including the Indian law that the father of the murdered man must kill the murderer. But first they sent a committee to consult the clergyman, whose approval being obtained, they made Toomalek sit down, and gave John a musket, with which he executed the judgment of private revenge and public law on the son of Molly.

Joe and Molly were present at the execution, buried the body themselves, and it is reported that Molly, who had but lately wept long and bitterly over the natural death of her other son, Muxawuxal, shed no tears for Toomalek, nor was ever heard to mention his name. During the War of the Revolution Joe was always on the side of the colonists; was a great admirer of Washington; boasted of a visit he once paid to the great father at Newburg on the Hudson and of a kind reception there, and was known to have such permanent hatred towards the British that he would never cross the Canada line even in following moose through the forests. His Indian friends could never persuade him to join the St. Francis tribe in Canada, nor when once they stole Molly and carried her there would he go after her. She came back and died. He outlived her, and growing very old, received a pension of $70 per annum from Vermont until his death in 1819. When he died the Newbury people did him honor, laid him in the north-east corner of the burying-ground, and discharged over his grave the last load which the old Indian had placed and left in his gun. Says Mr. Powers (the historian of the Coos country, from whose book I have condensed this story): "with Captain Joe fell the last of the Indians at Coosuck, that once fairy-land of long-slumbering generations."

You will see that the names "Joe's Pond" and "Molly's Pond" are sacred historical names. Some one will be trying to change them some day because they are not of pleasant sound. But they should stand.

We dined at Marshfield, drove on to Plainfield, and instead of keeping on to Montpelier turned southward, crossing high hills with far views of the mountains, and reached Barre at sunset.

As I entered the village an old friend greeted me. We had been together in many countries, and his greeting was the salutation of peace which is common in the Orient.

Why is it that English-speaking peoples of all the world have none of those beautiful forms of greeting when friends meet? It is because of this great lack in our language, or our customs, that travellers who have been in Oriental countries are fond of using Oriental salutations. The American or the Englishman, when he meets his dearest friends after a long or short separation, in ninety-nine cases out of a hundred asks him, "How do you do?" or "How are you?" Perhaps he varies it by saying, if surprised, "Why, John!" Lovers have no more tender phrase when they meet in the presence of friends than the same "How do you do?" The physician or the clergyman coming to the bedside of the sick man or woman, like all other friends, can only ask, "How do you do to-day?" or, "How do you find yourself?" or some other vague inquiry always beginning with "how."

It is otherwise in parting. We have good old phrases of benediction which we use, whether we mean them or not. Why not some like phrases for salutation in meeting, like the old Romans, "Good health to you;" or, best of all, that salutation which has been used in the Orient with uninterrupted succession for thousands of years, "Peace be with you."

What were the revisers of the Old Testament about when they failed to revise the King James translation of that salutation repeatedly occurring? When the prophet met the woman whose boy lay dead at home, he did not greet her in the vague phraseology of the Englishman or the American,

" Is it well with thee? Is it well with the child?" Nor did she answer with that cold word "Well." He said, "Is it peace with thee? Is it peace with the child?" and she said, with infinite calm and trust, "It is peace."

XIII

BOYS WITH STAND-UP COLLARS

WHAT boys those were! Looking about one in the Christmas-times in New York, and seeing the crowds of young people who are at home from school for the holidays, it is impossible not to contrast the boys of to-day in the city with those boys. This is not the pessimist's way of always thinking the old times better than the latter days. It is no imaginary contrast. It is simply the demand of the modern boy, which he makes on you wherever you meet him, to examine and pronounce judgment on him. He challenges your opinion. His mother sent him out into the street to challenge it. He is a work of art, and as such is set before you to be admired, with the expectation that you will look at him and pronounce on the quality of the art which has produced him. These little specimens of young humanity, with tight little trousers, tight little coats, tight little white chokers around their necks, little canes in their hands and little thoughts in their heads, are correct representatives of the boys that some modern mothers are bringing up for the next generation of men.

It is a melancholy fact, which no father who has daughters can fail to recognize, that the girls of to-day are in education and personal force of character much ahead of the boys. There are plenty of hearty, bright, brilliant, sensible girls. Society has not spoiled them, with all its frivolities.

Society is an essential part of this life. Those who abuse it with wholesale sweeping denunciations do not know what they are talking about. The purpose of education and life is happiness—here and hereafter. She who has been so educated that she is able to be happy and hopeful and to confer happiness and hopefulness on those around her—is well educated. This life and the other life are closely interwoven, and it is by no means necessary to abandon this life for the sake of getting ready for that. The duties of this life are present duties, and whatever be our social surroundings, whether in the informal associations of country society or in the settled formalities and splendid decorations of city society, there are duties which men and women owe to one another. Those who inveigh against the evils of society would do well to measure the certain results which would follow the abolition of that which they decry. Our civilization rests for its support on the splendors and luxuries of life far more than on the utilities. Our charities, hospitals, missions, all derive their support from the wealth which is the product of our social system. No mechanic, mason, carpenter, hod-carrier, artisan, tradesman, whatever his employment, whatever he produces or sells, would have a dollar to give to the church or the poor but for the fact that the rich wear rich apparel, live in gorgeous houses, give brilliant receptions, enjoy the splendor of modern social life.

In this social life, whether its brilliancy be that of intellectual gatherings, or of dress and formality, woman has right to rule supreme. There is no work of art on earth, ancient or modern, more beautiful, more worthy of admiration, than a well-dressed woman. If she were not a thing to be admired, the saint of old time, to whom were given visions of heaven, would not have likened the Holy City to a bride adorned. The pathway to the better country does not necessarily lie through the waste places of this life. Many saints there be who have walked it among all the splendors and allurements of society. Mostly, I think, women, not men. And in our own day, it is undeniable that the young women in society are in general the intellectual superiors of the young men. Some parents look solely for wealth in selecting husbands for their daughters; but I imagine these parents are more rare than is commonly believed. And it is certainly true that many judicious fathers and mothers, recognizing the ability of their daughters to be blessings and adornments of homes and of society, are sadly occupied in measuring the visible inferiority of the young men whom they see and estimate side by side with their daughters.

What boys those were! Can these little fellows, with tight collars and cravats at fourteen, ever make such men as those boys made? There is something wholly inconsistent with development of intellect in a tight stand-up collar around a boy's neck. Freedom of physical action is certainly essential to freedom of mind and thought. Fashion imposes on men in society formalities of dress. The rules of society are proper and obedience is necessary; otherwise society would degenerate and license destroy its system, which must be preserved. Therefore men in society must dress as the rules require, however ill be the taste which has made the rules. But boys are not in society; and it is a fearful blunder which mothers make in dressing their boys as if they belonged to a social system, or according to the rules of any such system, thus teaching them to demand such dress as they grow older, and to regard it as a governing consideration in life. Boys who dress in the style of some absurd-looking slips of humanity one meets nowadays can't possibly be boys. They are little automatons, mimicking the solemnities of mature life, caricaturing the sober realities of society.

What boys those were!—I say it again. The memory of them comes with the fresh brilliancy of a December Christmas wind out of the north, sharp, clear, with the sound of sleigh-bells and shouts. Are there any like them now? Doubtless plenty; but the modern schools, with gymnasiums for training the physical system, do not seem to turn out one in three, or one in a dozen, such boys as used to be in any high-class school in the country. The contrary is asserted. I don't believe it. Never did the system of old Greece, which classed athletics among the three great branches of education, make more noble specimens of young strength than our country schools did in old times, and perhaps now do. But these are never the boys that wear tight things around any of their muscles—above all, never boys that wear stiff stand-up collars habitually. To be a great boy is easier than to be a great man. It comes naturally with pure association, liberal use of muscles as well as mind, freedom of feeling which comes from freedom of clothing. It is easy to spoil what would be a great boy if let alone. Put him up to thinking much of how he looks when dressed to go out, and the boy will turn out next to worthless as a boy among boys, and have poor prospects as a man.

Perhaps I mistake those boys of old time, and the glow which invests them is the deceitful light that memory sometimes creates like a halo around the things we loved long ago. But there is no error in the estimate one must make of a large class of boys in modern cities. There is good stuff in them, but the vigor and force is taken out of it between the ages of eight and fifteen. They have by that time no independence of character; are, at their best, imitators, without self-reliance. It is a bad thing to make a boy's ambition to be measured by what other boys do, his ideas of taste controlled by other boys' ideas, his language and conversation reduced to the slang of a set of boys.

If you have no other guide in conducting your boy's life, good mother, take this: Give him something to remember; keep him from all that he would in mature life wish to forget. There is no more precious possession to the man than memories of boyhood. They grow more precious with advancing age. If it be possible, forbid in your boy's life that he shall ever look back from the serious years of maturity and have to say to himself, "What a little fool I was in those days!" All men remember follies, and the honest follies of a boy are pleasant memories, that one can laugh at and remember joyously. But deliberate follies persisted in from year to year, through all the sunniest years of life, are not pleasant to look back at; and saddest of all they will seem if the boy-man shall have to say, "I was a foolish boy because my parents made me one."

All this because of the group of country boys we saw at play in front of a school-house on the roadside. They were stout, healthy, happy boys, and some of them will be men of mark hereafter.

XIV

PILGRIMAGE ENDED

It is a windy night. Elsewhere it might be called a tempestuous night, but up in the north country of New Hampshire we are used to high winds, and this is only a gale, not a tempest. The forest is uttering thunderous voices, such as it always utters when arguing with the wind. You can find resemblances to any and every sound you ever heard in these forest sounds. Low voices in various tones mingle with the roar. Sitting here in the cabin, you will think them like whatever your mind happens to be directed towards. I have been reading a book; therefore I hear the sound of the surf on a reef, and the whistling of the wind through the cordage of a ship, and the cries of people in many tones. I have been reading an account of a traveller landing from a ship at the port of Jaffa—ancient Joppa—the seaport of Jerusalem. They call it a port, but it is no port. The steamer anchors in the offing. If the wind be off shore you can go safely enough through the break in the reef; if the wind be otherwise, and be only a little fresh, the landing is difficult, sometimes impracticable. Several times I have gone through the reef, and fought my way up the steps into the crowd of Turks, Arabs, and infidels on the shore street of that wretched Jaffa. The last time that I was there I did not go ashore. The day was memorable, and comes back in memory whenever, as now, I read of the experience of travellers on their way to the Holy City.

We were coming down the coast of the Levant on the Austrian Lloyds' steamer. The only first-class passenger on board besides ourselves was a Greek caloyer; but the deck of the ship was loaded with hundreds of poor pilgrims on their way to Jerusalem—a crowd of men, women, and children of various nationalities, mostly showing signs of extreme poverty, and all very far away from godliness in the matter of cleanliness. It was difficult to make one's way along the deck without treading on arms or legs or children. Why do those poor pilgrims always take such crowds of children to Jerusalem?

In the cabin all was pleasant. The steamer was of the first-class, and her table was of the best I ever saw at sea. It was in consequence thereof that I made the acquaintance of the priest, our only fellow-traveller; for at the dinner-table we sat down only five persons, of whom two were the captain and the ship's surgeon; and when I praised a dish, the latter spoke, saying, "We are proud of our table, and think we have the best cook but one in the Austrian Lloyds' service."

"Yes, he is certainly a great cook; but who is his superior?"

"His father, who is one of the oldest cooks in the service, and has six sons, all cooks in the service, and two daughters married to cooks in the service."

"A valuable family to the service," said a remarkably gentle and yet strong voice at my side, and I turned to look at the man who had just taken his place by me. He was a man of forty or forty-five, full six feet high, wearing the elevated black cap of the Greek Church. His face was singularly attractive and impressive, the features sharp cut, forehead high, complexion surprisingly white and pure, eyes dark, full of life and full of benevolence. It was a face to fall in love with. The expression of his eye as my glance met his was winning, and his whole appearance that of power and saintliness combined. Somewhat such a man I think was the Apostle John. It is rare to meet one whose look impresses you thus with the thought that this man is not of the world, worldly. I had prejudices against Greek monks and priests, for most of those that one meets in Egypt and Syria are ignorant, absolutely dirty in dress and person, and generally objectionable; but of this man I said at once he is a typical Caloyer, καλος γερος—a "beautiful elder" in the Church; and with a suddenness, of which I doubt not you remember examples in your experience among men, I yielded myself to the charm which drew me towards him. It soon appeared that he was a man of much learning as well as much experience among men, and our conversation, commenced at the dinner-table, continued on deck until late in the night.

Thrown by accident on a steamer loaded with Greek pilgrims, he found work to do, and he did it here as everywhere, on his Master's service. He seemed at once to know the case of every family and group among them; and though many were uncouth and by no means gentle in their manners, he was rapidly recognized by all, or most of them, as a good pastor, and was unwearying in his attention, especially to the sick and suffering, of whom there were not a few. When we came out from Beyrout to run down the Phœnician coast, we met a sirocco, and there is no storm more trying. Hot and fierce, the wind seemed to cut off your breath as with a red-hot sword, and all day long the blue seas went over the ship, half-drowning the miserable pilgrims who lay huddled in masses all over the deck. It was a brief luxury of rest when we ran under the lee of Mount Carmel and dropped anchor for an hour or two at Haifa.

It is memorable now, in connection with what

afterwards occurred, that we talked that evening of pilgrimages. He was making the pilgrimage. He had never seen Jerusalem, and was now devoutly going to the Sepulchre. Across the plain of Esdraelon, which touches the sea near Haifa, we looked at the huge slopes of Lebanon, and I tried to point out to him, among more distant mountains, the peaks of Tabor and Gilboa, the hills that are around Nazareth, and the dark summit of Little Hermon, which looks down on the blue beauty of the Sea of Galilee. And then we talked of pilgrims in old times, in all the ages, and spoke especially of the exceeding bitterness of their disappointment who, after long journeys across Europe and over the sea, reached the gates of Jerusalem, and when the Saracens forbade their entrance, lay down and died under the very walls, never having seen the Sepulchre.

The sun went down in white dust, the desert sand of Arabia flying over the sea before the sirocco, and the ship again plunged into the face of the tempest. In the morning at daybreak we anchored in the roadstead off Jaffa, two miles or so from the shore, and the first fierce jerk of the ship at her chain threatened to hurl everything out of her. What an anchorage that was! A tremendous sea was running. Under ordinary circumstances the captain would not have anchored, but would have gone on with his passengers to Alexandria. This is sometimes, often, the luck of those who seek to reach Jerusalem. But it lacked only a few days of the Greek Easter, the great day of the pilgrimage, and if carried on to Egypt, these hundreds of poor pilgrims would miss the chief object of their long journey. So the good Austrian officer anchored, and fired cannon to tell the Jaffa boatmen that it was for them to decide whether they would take the risk of coming out through the surf on the reef. We rolled and plunged and waited. About nine or ten o'clock, the wind seeming to draw a little more directly off shore, the shore boats began to appear and disappear, rising and falling on the great waves as they came towards the ship, and at length were alongside. It was a fearful business to get into them, the steamer rolling over almost on her beam ends at every sea. With long delay and much danger, boat after boat received a load of pilgrims and luggage, and one after another went tossing shoreward and safely passed the opening in the reef.

On board were left fifteen or twenty timid women and men who had not dared the fearful descent of the ship's ladder, and my friend, the priest, who had remained to the last to give them all his aid and comfort. There was one queer little old woman who passed the time in alternate shrieking, laughing, and crying. Ten times she essayed the ladder when the ship rolled to port, and rushed back or tumbled back on deck when the angle

changed and the bottom step was ten feet above
the boat. The priest gently encouraged her, but
in vain, and at last a sailor, watching his chance as
she once more shrieked and fell back, seized her
in his arms, rushed down the steps and tossed her
like a bundle into the boat. She was the last except my friend. I took his hand, and we parted
with many Oriental words of peace. He reached
the boat, took his seat on a bench in the middle,
and as she swung across the stern of the ship on a
long wave he bared his noble head, and with repeated waves of our hands, and words lost in the
storm, we exchanged the last salutations. He looked
like a pastor with his flock around him. Calm,
silent, his forehead swept with the fierce sirocco
wind which he was facing, I followed them with
my eyes, now on wave tops, now wholly lost to
sight. At length I used my glass—a fine marine
glass—it lies here to-night on the cabin table—and
with that I kept them steadily in view. The reef
was a white wall of foam dashing high into the air.
As they approached a narrow opening where a
darker sea indicated the passage, the waves grew
shorter. Their boat appeared and vanished in
quick succession. "Are they past the opening?"
"I cannot tell; I think they are just in it. The
sea is awful." And the words were not uttered
when in the field of my glass I saw a terrible vision.
The boat was lifted on a mass of water, it rose high,

and then suddenly I saw the bow thrown up, a hideous confusion of men and women and children among oars and baggage were hurled into the white surf on the reef, which leaped into the air triumphant, and I saw no more of them; only the upturned boat, floating, and tossed now and then into full view, swept northward along the shore, and finally went on the sandy beach in the breakers a half-mile north of the northern wall of the city.

So seeking Jerusalem that is below, before his pilgrim sandals had yet touched the soil of the beloved land, my newly-made and newly-lost friend, the good priest, found Jerusalem that is above, the mother of us all.

I have thought of him a thousand times since then, most frequently when in the forest on windy nights. In the roar of the mountain storm which rages around the cabin, mingled with the shrieks of the forest trees writhing and intertwining their giant arms, I recall that pale, calm face and commanding form as the boat sweeps shoreward on the great seas of the Mediterranean; and while I see him wave his hand, I can hear again and again and again, as I could not then hear what I knew he was saying, *Salame, salame, salame,* "Peace, peace, peace." And I know that in every tempest, on land or sea, the war of the elements is but a little agitation which to our weak sense seems great. The mountain stands calm, though my cabin shakes in the storm, and the surroundings which I have made seem ready to be swept away. And the Peace of Jerusalem—the peace that passes our understanding—the peace whose blessing he gave me across the sea when he waved his white hand to me in the sirocco blast — that peace is more calm than the mountain, more enduring than sea and shore, and abides forever in the City of Peace whither he went that morning through the tempest.

XV
NON-RESISTANCE

IT is very difficult for the honest advocate of the doctrine of non-resistance to live up to his principles. The duty of self-defence, the divinely-ordained right of the master of the house to forbid the spoiling of his goods, the self-evident law which commands every one to defend the weak against the oppressing strong, these are requirements which a man may honestly try to ignore, but which, unless he be a coward, he will never succeed in ignoring when the trial of his faith comes. The sturdy non-resistant, sturdy of soul as of body, who has yesterday defended a little child from the attack of a dog, will to-day defend the same child from the attack of a brute in shape of man, and to-morrow will defend his country and government against enemies.

In one of the villages through which we drove yesterday was once a society called a non-resistance society. Its members were men and women, good, honest, well-meaning people all of them. Its history was brief, but not altogether uneventful. It was strong in its principles, but it was from time to time enfeebled by the failures of its members in practical life; and when at last the Civil War began it ceased to exist, because some of its members went to fight for the Union, and all the others encouraged them to go and rejoiced in their patriotism.

While it existed, and indeed long before it was organized, Jabez Dickinson was known in the whole town as a steadfast advocate of the doctrine of submission without forcible resistance.

He was the village merchant, kept the village store, where he sold everything from silk ribbons to tallow candles and sugar candies. He was not a deacon, but he was always named and known as Deacon Jabe, because there was never known a man who more firmly, boldly, and consistently asserted and practiced the doctrines of the Christian life. Universally loved and respected by the people, old and young, he had led a long life of peace and quiet, doing good and getting good. And during this life he had been an unwavering non-resistant. He was not much of a talker. He seldom preached. But in the store, where it was the custom of the men of the community to gather, especially on Saturday evenings, the nickname deacon had been given to him for years, and thence had travelled through the community. Seldom volunteering opinions, he was often appealed to for the decision of mooted questions. And if you do not know it, I can tell you that in the country store there are daily discussions of questions, moral, philosophical, religious, and practical, in which at least as much average good sound sense and logical power is developed as in any meeting of any of the modern scientific associations, British or American. Always, however, Deacon Jabe had laid down and adhered to his non-resistance principles, and this in the face of much provocation to think and act otherwise. Many indignities he had suffered from fellows of the baser sort, insults and personal wrongs, always taking them meekly and without resentment. In all the town there was but one supporter of his radical views, and he often wished he was free from that ally; for Miss Almira Smith was a cantankerous talker and fighter, doing with her tongue a perpetual war, offensive and defensive, while she proclaimed the sinfulness of physical offence or defence with any other muscles or member of the human body. For, after all, it is but a question of muscles, and the non-resistant who forbids blows with the fist is often a conscientious dealer of deadly blows with the voice.

The deacon had received much and sore provocation that week from Silas Maxwell, the town bully, a fellow of powerful structure, who rejoiced in his ability to whip any man in the county. And he had fought many battles, not in sport, with invariable victory. My story would be too long were I to recite the talk on Saturday evening in the store when Silas nagged Jabez and insulted him again and again, presuming, and boasting that he presumed, on the deacon's non-resistance, which Silas said was nothing but cowardice. "He don't resist bekase he daresent resist," said the bully, walking across the store and helping himself to a chunk of tobacco, at the same moment opening a huge knife wherewith to cut off a mouthful.

Little Katie Wheeler was the deacon's granddaughter, a lovely child, the joy of his life, sole descendant of his dead wife and daughter. Katie was a sad invalid, but she had a well mind, never ill, never sickly. All day long she was in and out of the store, always breezy and cheery, making perpetual spring-time in the life of the lonesome man. Her little chair stood where in the evenings she sat till her grandfather closed the door and she walked home with him. Every one loved Katie—even Silas Maxwell, brute though he was. As Silas took the tobacco in his hand, Katie sprang from her chair and snatched it away from him, saying, "Silas Maxwell, you sha'n't steal granther's tobacco any more." The child's impulsive act and clear ringing voice were greeted with a shout from the fifteen or twenty villagers in the store. The act, the word "steal," and the approving shout roused the devil in Silas, and, seizing Katie by the arm, he uttered a brutal oath as he raised his right hand with the open knife to strike.

Jabez had kept his eye on the man, and up to this instant had been struggling to keep down what he believed to be his sinful desire to silence the other's insolence with earthly weapons. Now, as he saw the knife raised, he was a converted man. Well was it for Katie that her grandfather in the long-forgotten days of his sinful youth had been mighty in battle, power residing in the muscles of his arms and shoulders, for which he had been famous when Silas Maxwell was a child. The deacon's legs were like steel springs, and without waiting for his mind to direct them, they of their own free will launched him like a rock from a catapult across the store. The shoulder and arm acted next, for the deacon always declared that it was the physical body God had given him which acted for itself when the closed fist dealt on the bridge of Silas Maxwell's nose an awful blow. The bully reeled backward one, two, three short steps and fell, full length, over a keg of nails.

Jabez stood silent, while Silas gathered himself up. He knew what was coming, and now he reasoned within himself, swiftly but sufficiently. And when the huge fellow rushed at him intent on crushing him, the old skill (he said it was learned in the devil's service) now came to him for the Lord's service in the defence of himself and the child and the just punishment of that ruffian. Silas Maxwell had for the first time met his master. Those trip-hammer blows of Jabez Dickinson's tremendous fist live in the village traditions. There were but three, or at the most four, of them, with the right arm first, with the left arm second, the other arm stopping the puny thrusts of the bully. And so it came about that Jabez drove Silas across the store till he stood with his back to the window, open to the floor. When he had him there he dealt one more and final blow, right between the big man's eyes, a blow backed up with a continuous thrust from all the weight of his body, which threw the ruffian off his feet, heels overhead through the window. The mill-race ran close under that window. The deacon knew it, and had been thinking of it all the forty seconds or less between the first rush of Silas and his final exit. "Go out, some on ye, and take him out. I kinder think he's got enough of it," said Jabez, very calmly, as he sat down and took Katie on his knees and kissed her.

There was silence and awe in the store for a few moments. Then some one came in and said that Silas reckoned he had got enough, and had gone home. Silas was converted then and thenceforward.

Not so the deacon. He was, like all non-resistants under like circumstances, in some danger of relapse into his old folly. I have not space to relate at length how his new sentiments became fixed. It came about in this way: Miss Smith made a descent on him the next day and poured out on him the vials of her peculiarly unpleasant wrath for "goin' back on non-resistance." He listened in silence. Again and again, and again, alone and in presence of whatever people might be in the store, that inexpressible and intolerable female rated Jabez. And Jabez became hardened. At last he deliberately made up his mind that resistance to a male bully like Silas had been a religious duty, and, as a corollary, that resistance, duly measured for the case, to a female bully like Almira Smith, would be a virtue. So he prepared a trap, and one day when Almira was coming down the street, and Jabez knew that her entrance and assault on him were as certain as foreordination, he set the trap.

"Jabez," said the sharp voice, as its owner entered the store, "Jabez Dickinson," it repeated, as she crossed the floor. "Look out, Almiry," said the deacon; "stop jist there or you'll spill somethin'!"

"What are you talkin' about, Deacon Jabez Dickinson," said the keen, piercing voice. "I've come in because I can't find it in me to pass by without warnin' you—" At that moment there descended around Almira Smith a cloud of fine black pepper. It began gently, and she interrupted her tirade with a sneeze. She tried to resume, but the more she tried the more she sneezed, and the clouds gathered thicker around her. Sneezing and dignity are incompatible. Continuous sneezing is incompatible with self-respect or self-admiration. Almira had no idea of charging her convulsive affliction to the deacon's new doctrine of resistance to vocal and other physical assaults. She abandoned the field; she sneezed along the road home; she sneezed all night.

And Jabez chuckled, and kept his secret, and lived, and is living now, a sensible man. "Ye see," he said, in confidence, "I could 'a' stood Silas, and if he'd 'a' come back I'd 'a' told him I was sorry. Silas came in, and before I got a chance he told me he was sorry, and I kind o' concluded I had been doin' right. But the nat'ral man couldn't stand Almiry Smith."

XVI

SONGS OF THE AGES

I HAD driven into the village the evening before. I knew no one there. The inn was clean and neat; the stable was good; my horses and myself had a quiet Sunday rest. In the church in the morning was the usual slim congregation, thirty or forty people. Notice was given of a "service of song" at the school-house in the evening.

It was a small room, and crowded. The kerosene lamps gave a dim light and a vile smell. There were more people there than had been in the church in the morning. The room was very hot. A lady presided at the melodeon, facing the assembly. For a while she led, by playing one and another tune of her own selection. Then she asked any one to propose hymns or songs, and voices would be heard calling out this or that page of the hymn or song book they were using. When a page was so called she would at once turn to it, and they sang together; it was good singing. They knew the words and tunes, and sang with spirit and appreciation. There were some harsh, some reedy, some sweet voices. All together were melodious. It was a pity, as it is everywhere in the north country, that the words they sang were mostly doggerel rhymes which have become popular of late years, and have demoralized the hymnology of many parts of the country.

At length the lady left the melodeon, and a man's voice broke the temporary silence which followed. He was praying. I sat near the door, and could see no faces. No one knelt or bowed a head. It is not the custom up there. His prayer was short, simple in diction, several times ungrammatical, but it was heard, I doubt not, for it was earnest, eloquent, beseeching in its tone; the prayer of one who felt deeply the load of this world's weariness, and whose faith was absolute in the promise of his Master, which he cited: "Thou didst say that if we would come to Thee we should have rest. Give us rest, O Lord! Amen."

Then there was silence again, and a woman's voice broke it. It was not a pleasant voice. It was somewhat nasal, a little sharp and shaky, and perhaps querulous in tone. She only sang a word or two alone, and then another, and then all the gathering joined her in that wonderful hymn, "Art thou weary, art thou languid?"

There was something very moving, very thrilling in the utterance of the hymn by that group of up-country people. They were one and all hard-working men and women, to whom life is the perpetuation of the curse—labor for bread. The touching words in which Dr. Neale clothed the sentiment of the hymn entered into their souls. There was all the eloquence of which the human voice is capable in the way they sang, with suppressed, inquiring, almost doubting voice,

> "If I still hold closely to Him,
> What hath He at last?"

and a swelling triumph of assurance as they poured out the response,

> "Sorrow vanquished, labor ended,
> Jordan passed!"

Music is not to be measured by any arbitrary rules of the musical world. I have often heard vesper song in St. Peters. I have heard a Te Deum in Notre Dame, sung to God — and to the emperor and empress. There was never music which ascended to Heaven more musical than that song in the little New Hampshire schoolhouse.

As I walked along the dark country road in a drizzling rain, stumbling over stones, and once bringing up short against the end of an open gate, I heard the voices of young people coming behind me. One said: "Girls, who wrote that last hymn we sung?" "I'm sure I don't know," said another.

It was not exactly the thing for a stranger to speak out in the darkness and tell them. But I went on to my inn, thinking on this wise:

It is the fashion to speak ill of the ages called Dark Ages. By reason of the bitterness of theological controversy the Protestant world is very generally imbued with the idea that for a long and somewhat indefinite period before the sixteenth century the European world and all the rest of the world was in a state of sin and iniquity; degraded in intelligence, in arts and in religion; that everybody went to the bad. The myth of the Dark Ages is still believed in.

Out of those ages we have an abundant brilliant literature, as glorious art, as pure religion as our own age can boast. There was no more darkness then than now. There were weak men and great men, good men and wicked men, in the church and out of it, then as now.

It is the fashion to ridicule the hermits and monks of the early ages. There were dirty hermits and dirty monks abhorring water and rejoicing in uncleanliness. We meet such men, called clergy in Roman and in Protestant churches, nowadays. But there were monks and hermits of another sort, too, as there are Roman and Protestant clergymen now, men of holy life and labor, whose works have followed and will follow them on earth and forever hereafter.

From the dark road through the little New Hampshire village my vision went to a great gorge in the mountains where the Kedron pours its floods in the rainy season, plunging downward from Jerusalem to the Dead Sea. The rocky walls of the narrow gorge, broken and irregular, rise two or three hundred feet above the noisy bed of the stream. Here, in caverns and hollows of the rocks, perching like eagles on the sides of the chasm, one and another man, weary of the world, came and made for himself a hermitage, a hole, with what shelter the overhanging cliff might give him. After a while pathways, difficult and dangerous, along the ledges, led from one's miserable abode to that of another. So a community was formed, a sort of hermit village, and its fame went abroad; for there were great men, learned men, noble men, who gave up the world and sought repose and oblivion in the gorge of the Kedron. Thus grew the famed monastery of St. Sabas, once the most powerful monastery in the Eastern Church. Here in the eighth century came John of Damascus, last and not least of the Greek Fathers of the Church; and Cosmas of Jerusalem, Cosmas the melodious, poet and holy man, whose songs are sung in all lands where Christians sing. And with them was one Stephen, of whom we know little more than that he was a Sabaite, and hence is called St. Stephen the Sabaite. These all wrote in Greek. St. John Damascene wrote the

"Resurrection Hymn," which is known in Dr. Neale's translation:

" From death to life eternal,
From earth unto the sky,
Our Christ hath brought us over
With hymns of victory."

I wonder who was Stephen. He lived long, long ago—more than a thousand years ago. He was a man, and therefore he had sorrow and labor, and was heavy laden. He found rest, remembering the Master's invitation. He remembered the very words of it, as St. Matthew had recorded them, "Come unto me all ye that labor;" κοπιοντες was the word, "Ye laboring ones." He wrote an exquisitely simple and beautiful song beginning Κοπον τε και καματον: "labor and weariness"—and it touched the hearts of the good Christians of that and all the after ages in the Eastern Church. Yes, my friend, there were good Christians in the Eastern and in the Western Church, in all those times. Shake off the superstition that has enthralled you about the Church, and don't any longer imagine that all the people that have lived in Europe from apostolic times down to Luther's day are damned. You may find in heaven as large a proportion of souls out of what you call the Dark Ages as out of this age. There is no more sign of the millennium now than there was then.

It was not a great many years ago that Dr. Neale translated, or perhaps rather reproduced the sentiment of the hymn of Stephen the Sabaite in our tongue. And it entered the hearts of English speaking and singing and praying people, and touched the hearts of many who had not sung or prayed before; so that now all over the world they sing:

> "Art thou weary, art thou languid,
>   Art thou sore distressed?
> 'Come to me,' saith One, and coming,
>   Be at rest!"

I do not think there is any subject more worthy the philosopher's consideration than this presented to me in the school-house in a New Hampshire village by the dim light of two kerosene lamps, listening to the voices of weary men and women singing the song which Stephen the Sabaite wrote, a thousand years ago, in the deep gorge where the Kedron pierces the wilderness, hurrying down to the Sea of Death. If I did not believe in any God I should feel bound to inquire into that sameness of human character, suffering, wearying, wanting—the same in old Palestine, the same in Russia, Greece, Asia, Europe, America, and that oneness with which the monks of St. Sabas and the young girls of New Hampshire hold firm and unwavering the faith that was delivered to the saints.

XVII

IGNOTUS

THE road was across an open country. The hills which skirted the western horizon were wooded to their summits; only one massive peak of bare rock rose above the fringe of trees and stood out strong and almost black against the evening sky. The valley through which I was driving was very rich and fruitful. The farms were well kept, the farm-houses neat and comfortable, the barns and out-houses indicating by their appearance the thrifty character of the agricultural population. There was for several miles no house which did not stand in a group of trees, whose great trunks and spreading branches were proof of considerable age in the home location under their shade. At length I came where on each side of the road was a row of elms, large old trees, and soon to a group of houses. The road widened and parted into two roads, with a broad green between them. The elms were more abundant, scattered here and there on the green. A small church, with rows of horse-sheds behind it, a house which could not be mistaken for any other than the parsonage, a store in front of which hung the sign "Post-office," and about a dozen other houses formed the village.

Before we reached the church the road passed the church-yard. A low stone-wall separated it from the road-side foot-path. It was easy, as the horses walked, to read the inscriptions on many headstones. It is always interesting to do this, for the mere sake of the names, both the surnames and the Christian names. I have given you lists of peculiar names thus perpetuated, which I have found in country graveyards. One acquires the habit of catching a name quickly, even at a distance and on a discolored stone. So as we passed along I read aloud one and another and another name, most of them old Bible names, now and then a strange name, doubtless a home invention.

I read aloud Samuel, Hepzibah, Bezaleel, Marina, Isaiah, Ichabod, Ignotus—, and as I read the last name I said "Whoa" to the horses. Surely that could not be a man's name. I leaped over the low wall and went to the grave which was near it. The stone was a low, black-slate slab, on which green and gray lichens were growing in such density that the original color was invisible except near the top where the slab was cleaned, evidently with care, so as to leave the word "IGNOTUS" plainly legible. And there was no other word on the stone.

Of course I was interested in this; and you will

readily imagine the succession of thoughts which it aroused. At first I took it to be the grave of one who, possibly knowing of the celebrated MISERIMUS inscription, had directed the expression of utmost humility to be placed over his ashes. While I was pondering on this an elderly gentleman came along the road, and seeing where I was standing, paused at the wall. As I looked up he fixed his eyes on me with an expression which said as plainly as words could say, "You would like to know what that inscription means?" I took him at his word—or at his eyes—and said, "Can you tell me anything about this stone?"

"Everything about the stone," was the reply, "very little about the dust that lies below it."

"Then no one knows whose grave this is?"

"Precisely so. The inscription and the grave-mound together tell all that can be told. The mound is long. The inscription is in the masculine. The two tell you that an unknown man lies below."

"May I ask who ordered the stone and the inscription—for I fancy most if not all the other inscriptions here are in the English language?"

"Yes, most of them; not always the best of English. I had this stone cut and set here. The stone-cutter didn't understand it. As a rule the people around here don't know what it means. Pardon me. I should introduce myself. I am the pastor of these people. Most of the sleepers hereabouts were of my flock. The living are my care now. These are in God's care."

"And this man—he was not of your flock, I take it?"

"No and yes. If the shepherd find a stray sheep in ill condition, he should surely care for the poor beast, and make it one of his flock till it goes to its master. So it was with this man and myself. He came into the village one dark night forty years ago. He was ragged, dirty, old. There was a tavern then over yonder. The landlord found him lying on the ground in front of his door. He was a good Samaritan, my old friend Hezekiah Bolter; yonder is his grave. God give him rest! He took the man in and sent for the doctor, and the doctor sent for me. But the man was past help from either of us. He showed no signs of consciousness until after some powerful stimulus which the doctor administered. Then he murmured a little. But he never opened his eyes. We stayed by him for hours. His murmurs took the form of short sentences, and these sentences were Latin. When they were complete I recognized some of them. They were familiar passages, now from Virgil, now Horace, now Juvenal. Were these memories of his boyhood, or were they the utterances of a mind familiar, as a teacher's might be, with the Latin authors used in schools and colleges? We did not discuss the matter then, but much afterwards; and while the doctor maintained that the man was probably a teacher, I held to the theory that he was recalling memories, quoting passages which he had not thought of for years. We had, neither of us, anything on which to base our arguments; which is all the better for freedom of discussion. He died before morning. There was nothing in the pockets of his ragged clothing. We could learn nothing about him, and there was nothing to do but to bury him. I ordered the stone; the doctor paid for it."

Such was in brief, almost in full, the narrative which the good old man gave me, as we walked along to the gate by the side of the church, he on the outside, I on the inside of the wall. We met at the gate, and I ventured there to take his hand. The words he had spoken were a simple story, but there was a quaintness and earnestness in his tones which had quite won me. I am not sure that there are many pastors now (I know there is one) whom you would expect to hear of as staying all night by the side of a dying pauper, hoping for one interval of consciousness wherein he might give to the poor soul light for the dark road on which it was travelling. I ventured somewhat more, after I had taken his hand. I said, " And when you buried him you prayed for him."

" Why do you think that?"

"Because just now you prayed for the repose of the soul of Hezekiah Bolter."

"Ah, so I did; and so I do very often. What would be the lonesomeness, what would be the intolerable bereavement of this life of mine, of life in this world for you or me or any one, if we believed the dead were all gone out of the universe of God, out of his reach, into an unknown domain where they do not need a God, and prayer is vain. I have been in the cure of souls here for almost fifty years. The catalogue of those for whom it has been my duty to labor and to pray is larger on these stones and in these unmarked graves than in my list of the living. I never gave them up while they were here. I never gave up praying for them when they went out of the reach of my care."

"And it seems to me you care somewhat for their graves. I suppose it is your care which has kept that word "Ignotus" so legible."

"Yes. I have never passed that grave without saying to myself, 'Ignotus, Ignotus; who was he, who is he, where did he go? I don't know, but God knows. Lord have mercy on him!'"

As I drove on in the gathering twilight I considered what I had heard. There was something very pathetic in the story of the ragged wanderer who had left all that had been his in some part of the world and died unknown. But it is much the same with all of us. It is only a question of time how soon the memory of every man's name and the place of his burial will be forgotten. If you look back two hundred years you will astonish yourself by finding how few graves of the dead of two centuries ago are known by monument. If you go back a thousand years the number is very small. If you seek the graves of mighty men or renowned women of the more ancient time, say three thousand years ago, you will find, except in Egypt, few if any besides the cave of Machpelah at Hebron and the tomb of Rachel on the way-side between Jerusalem and Bethlehem.

And the names of men are forgotten. They are merged in other and strange sounds. It is not at all certain that our pronunciation of those which have been handed down to us in phonetic characters is remotely correct For all purposes of identification you might as well call the great Macedonian Smith or Thompson as Alexander, pronouncing the word "Alexander" as moderns pronounce it. The Saracens call it Iskander. They are as near right as we are. But it is not alone the names which vanish. The greater the man the more certain it is that a doubting generation will arise who will pronounce the name and the man creatures of imagination, pure myths. Homer has but a shadowy existence as a person. The greatest name in history is that of Moses, giver of laws not only to Israel but to the whole race of civilized men to-day. And there are plenty of men of this age in which folly flourishes, who deny that there ever was a Moses. So the time may come when Washington will be the name of a shadow as unsubstantial as that of William Tell, and men will find in the fact that many peoples have legends of great and good leaders satisfactory evidence that no one of them ever had such a leader in veritable flesh.

XVIII

SEEKING A BETTER COUNTRY

IT was certainly as beautiful a spot for a home as one could find in this world. A rolling country, where the hills were sometimes crowned with maple forests in autumnal splendor of colors, sometimes cultivated to and over their ridges, yellow cornfields glowing with vast heaps of orange-colored pumpkins, pasture lands in which good cattle were feeding leisurely, brush lots crimson with sumach, except where rich blue asters made spots of the earth to look like spots of the sky.

But its beauty had not caused it to be thickly inhabited, had not even kept the population here which had once found homes in the valley; for as my horses walked slowly up the hill road we approached a house which, at a little distance off, looked picturesque and pretty, but as we came nearer was found to have only the beauty of ruin. It was a deserted farm-house.

There is sometimes beauty in ruin. Nature occasionally takes hold of the works of men's hands and shapes and decorates them to be very beautiful.

This old house had been a low story-and-a-half tenement, painted red. The red had faded and been washed into a score of tints, which only old tapestries and embroideries can match. Wild-cherry bushes, growing close around it, were trying to match them, and in trying made with their leaves very delicate and very surprising variations and contrasts. There was a spot of brilliant color which caught my eye long before I reached the house, and when I came up to it I discovered that a young maple had sprung up in the shattered door-step, and filled the doorway with its foliage, mostly of a like color with the house, only there was a bunch of leaves at the top, all as golden as gold.

Deserted farm-houses in New England are all alike in the most prominent features, generally resembling each other in many minute details. For the life in them was very much the same, and the life in the house gives specific character to the surroundings. The worn spot on the little piazza of the kitchen end, or L, is again and again visible, the spot where the farmer sat down daily for a little while when he took the very short rest which the farmer can afford to give himself in daylight. The marks on the inside of the window-seat are almost always there, made by the broken mugs and teapots and the cans and boxes in which his wife kept her flowers growing when frost drove them in-doors for the winter. Her garden is always there, and I know a place where I go and gather roses sometimes from bushes in a dense tangle, which were the garden roses of a farm-house that utterly vanished more than fifty years ago.

I drove on, still slowly uphill, and after a little saw the customary burial-ground, enclosed by a stone-wall, only a few rods from the road-side. Going to it I found four upright stones, and on one of them read a name, and an inscription which was somewhat startling: "But now they desire a better country."

Why do so many people make the mistake of expecting to find that better country by going off on railways? There is nowhere on earth a better country than this Northern New England country. When we get a reasonable amount of common-sense into legislatures and law-makers; when they get to realizing what a good country theirs is, and how good it can always be if they will preserve the glory of their forests from the axe and the purity of their streams from the saw-mill, it will be safe for any one to make a home in it for the time he must spend among the things that are uncertain.

Vermont and New Hampshire are becoming wide-awake to the extensive abandonment of farms and the gradual decrease of the best element in the population. The people are inquiring into the cause, with a view to finding a cure for the disease. It is a disease, and it is a disease which affects the community and the State by affecting individuals.

The inscription on that gravestone suggests the explanation of the disease. Those old people who are never going to travel off in search of a new home in the Far West were contented and happy enough in the red farm-house, looking for a better country beyond all seas, all possibilities of travel in the flesh. Later generations were not contented. Life was hard, and they thought to find a place where it would be easier. They went to a large town, to a city, to the West. It is beyond a doubt that they went to less happiness, to harder labor, with smaller reward. Not one in ten bettered his condition by the going. If you had known the personal history of as many country families who have moved away from the old places as I have known, you would understand why I am so ready to affirm that the great body of New England emigrants who have gone away from these farms have done worse than they would have done had they remained in the old homes.

Is it probable that the efforts now made to turn the tide of emigration and lead it into instead of out of New Hampshire and Vermont will succeed?

Why not? The land is fruitful and beautiful. The climate is wholesome and enjoyable. What is there to keep people away? Nothing, except that vague idea which is so universally deceptive that the better country, where one may grow rich with ease, may live well without much labor, lies far off at the end of a railway or a steamer journey.

There are some characteristics of American families in which they differ greatly from people of other countries. One of these is in their ideas of what form the necessaries of comfortable life. That which goes to the daily support of a humble family in America would support in luxury two or three or more families in the same social position in old countries. There are a hundred considerations which an American has in selecting a home which no European would stop to think of. I do not find fault with these, but they are to be regarded in seeking the causes of depopulation of portions of the country.

Contentment with a moderate enough is not an American characteristic. It ceases in a few years to characterize Europeans who come over here to settle. The "enough" includes too many things which are not necessities. ˙Look at a practical illustration: There are great numbers of American families in cities who are in what are called reduced circumstances. Men, women, sometimes husbands and wives, have but small incomes. They have a hard time to get food and clothing in the position and with the surroundings to which they have been accustomed. They suffer; their lives are full of struggling anxiety, pains, too often debts. They are unfitted for work, and work, if they were able to do it, is not easy to get. Thousands of these persons cling to life in the city, where rents are high, where food is costly, where the requirements of dress seem to demand much expense. Now at the same time you have the broad country, especially New Hampshire and Vermont, with these facts: The average expense of living of a family is not $500 a year; and this furnishes better and more abundant food, better and more clothing, better everything that men and women need, than can be found anywhere else in the world. You can hire a house for $100 a year in the country which is more roomy and comfortable than any house you can hire for $1000 anywhere within miles of Madison Square. You can get better board the year round in country places at $3, $4, and $5 a week than you can get in a city for $13, $14, or $15.

But if you suggest to the persons struggling on small incomes in city life that they go to the far-off country villages of New England to live and be happy, they shrink with apprehensions they cannot define from what seems miserable exile. I am not the one to make light of those desires, tastes, habits of life which form the comforts and shape the pleasures of all of us. No one can be happy for any one else. But if the people who cling to life in cities and expensive towns could be persuaded to consider with common-sense the question whether, after all, life in the country, with its abundant enjoyments and employments, and its small expense, is not the life they ought to adopt, it is probable that we should see a beginning of the repeopling of abandoned farms, and a new growth of a valuable population. A new generation might grow up to love home well enough to live and die in it.

It is not at all probable that the New England States will recall to their homes the same people, or call to them the same kind of people, who have left them. A new age has begun for all the eastern country. Wealth has increased in cities. The custom of having a country as well as a city home is largely on the increase. Before many years all parts of the country which are healthy and attractive will draw purchasers of lands for country homes. Where a few will seek such homes in fashionable localities for society pleasures, hundreds will seek them in more economical and quite as enjoyable places. More and more families will go into the country for the whole year. More and more men will retire from active business on small fortunes, instead of remaining in it to increase them, with the hundred to one chances of coming to grief and losing all. People of moderate means, and people of wealth, too, will learn how much nobler is a race of children brought up in the country than a race brought up in the city. And, to bring this to a close, the man who can count on an income of $800 a year while he has a family to support and care for, will be wise enough to go where he can buy a house and fifty or a hundred acres of land for $10 or $20 an acre, and live like a prince on his own estate from its produce, with an outside income of six or seven hundred. But even there he must work. The better country than the city is beyond doubt the free land of fields and forests. But work and weariness he must have forever on this soil of earth, nor will there be work without weariness anywhere until he shall reach the better country far away, which the inhabitants of the old red farm-house desired and I hope found.

XIX

A WINTER NIGHT'S ERRAND

THIS is the story which the doctor told me.

Ezekiel Crofton's farm was on the slope of the hill, two miles in a straight line from the village. But to reach it you had to go more than two miles down the valley, and a long one up the hill road. A deep ravine, wherein flowed a noble trout stream, cut off the farm from more direct communication with the village. But the farm-house, with its barns and out-houses, was a conspicuous object in the landscape, as seen from the back windows of the doctor's library.

There was sickness at the farm. Ezekiel's wife and Susie's mother lay ill, and the doctor had left her late in the afternoon with no little anxiety. But he had other patients, for it was a sickly winter. So Susie was instructed what to do if her mother grew worse. It was of no use to give Ezekiel orders. He was crazy. Trouble like this had never entered the farm-house before. Susie was to watch her mother, and report by a simple telegraph. The doctor set the tall clock by his watch. At ten o'clock, at midnight, and at two o'clock, if her mother should be worse, or if certain indications appeared, Susie was to burn a blaze of straw on the snow-bank in front of the house. The doctor would see it and drive out.

It was a cold night and the moon was young. The snow lay three feet deep on a level. A slight thaw, followed by a freeze, had left a glassy crust over everything. Then three inches of light snow had fallen without wind over this crust. It was after dark when the doctor reached home that night, and he was a weary man. Did I say he lived alone in his house? Yet not alone, for one who had been its light until a few years before never seemed to him absent from it. And though now, as he sat before the big fire, no one sat visibly by him, there was a cheery look on his face, just as there used to be when he sat there and talked to her. It is a wonderful joy, that which some hearts have, of living with those they love, whether gone away on a visit, or gone across what men call the river of death.

Dinner was on the table. Jupiter (son of Jupiter, who was also son of Jupiter, slave of the doctor's grandfather in that same village) stood while his master ate and drank. He never believed in the relationship between Burgundy and gout; and many a bottle of good sound wine of the Wind-mill Vineyard found its way from his cellar to the lips of the sick poor. The valley was a rich one, but the poor are always and everywhere. Would that such physicians with such cellars were equally abundant.

"Watch Mr. Crofton's farm from five minutes before to five minutes after ten, and again at midnight," said he to Jupiter. And the dark eyes set in ebony could be perfectly trusted.

The doctor was asleep on a lounge when midnight passed. There had been no signal from the farm. At two he stood at the back window and saw the blaze flash up from Susie's bonfire, for the poor girl was frightened and heaped the straw high. By the successive flashes he knew that she was throwing it on in armfuls, and that there was great trouble and fear at the farm-house.

The weather had changed. It was still cold but cloudy, and a snow-storm was hastening on. There were plenty of horses in the stable, and two powerful sorrels plunged out of the gate-way and down the broad village street, bringing up with a fierce rattle of the bells in front of the stone house near the church where lived the clergyman. He, too, was ready, for he had received warning from the doctor in the early evening and had watched. I am tempted to speak of him, that man whose memory is cherished by so many, who lived and died for those over whom he was appointed. But there is no space here. They two were men after one another's hearts. Happy the village with such a pair of doctors.

And now the wintry part of the story begins. For as they started a gust of wind met them, whirling the light snow which lay on the frozen crust. When they left the well-beaten village street and took the road down the valley a stiff gale was blowing. The track had been cut down like a deep canal between two banks, and the drift of the light snow which lay on the crust was fast filling it. It grew darker, for the moon was just setting, and it began to snow heavily. The runners cut deep in the hard pack. The horses were well used to such work, but there are impossibilities on roads before the best teams, and they found the first of these when the sorrels plunged into a heavy drift at the fork of the road where you turn up towards Ezekiel Crofton's. Thus far they had come at little faster than a walk, but for a few rods the horses had found light pulling and were on a swift trot when they plunged into this drift which lay diagonally across the road, full six feet deep. Down they went, while the doctors and the robes went in a confused mass over on the crust at the road-side.

No one was hurt, and at the voice of their master, who was at their heads in an instant, the sorrels recognized the situation and stood up. The drift was wide as well as deep, and the men righted the sleigh, gathered up the scatterings, then broke a road through the drift by trampling, and led the horses through and around the sharp turn into the hill road. All was made right, and they went on now very slowly; for the whole track was filled to the level of the banks, and the track on this less travelled road was narrow, and had been imperfectly broken before the new drift filled it. A hundred yards from the turn the left runner rose over a lump, caught the hard bank at the side, and lifted the sleigh so gently but so swiftly that as the doctor said "Whoa" he found himself lying in deep snow, a buffalo robe over him, and the minister on the buffalo robe. The horses had heard the word and stopped. This was a simple upset, a common enough affair to both of them. But a trace-hook had torn out, and it took ten minutes to mend it, for now they missed the lantern which had not been recovered at the first place of emptying the sleigh.

I will not dwell on the many incidents of that struggle, which the doctor related with keen enjoyment of the memory. It was a serious piece of business then. Sometimes it would have been ludicrous, but for the solemn errand that took them out in that tempestuous night among the hills. The storm increased, and the snow fell fast and deep and drifted into heaps. Again and again they were upset until they ceased to count the times. Now they went ahead and broke the way on foot for the horses. Now they took the horses out of the sleigh, mounted and rode them a little way to break road, and returned for the sleigh. Many good reasons forbade abandoning it. They were more than two hours on the half-mile between the fork of the roads and the first farm-house. Here they roused the people and held a consultation. Farmer Brown had six oxen in a stable a quarter of a mile off the road. He and his boys went for them. It took an hour or more to get them to the house, and the boys came near perishing. But who would not have worked that night, at any risk, to get the parson and the doctor to the bedside of Mrs. Crofton? The six oxen were put into the road, and driven up the hill through the drifts. Slowly and with infinite toil, shouting and encouragement, they floundered on. The sorrels followed in the track they broke. It stopped snowing, with the atmosphere far below zero, as the gray dawn came, and it was broad daylight when they entered the back gate of the Crofton farm-yard.

The roadway to the door crossed a hillock in front of the house, and the wind had swept it clean of drift. The horses sprang up the apparently clear track, but at the very summit again the left runner flew high and the last upset was accomplished. In full view of the windows, as if it were a circus show, the two doctors shot into the air and clutched each other before they struck the glassy surface of the hillock. They struck in a slanting fall and slid to the verge of the short but sharp descent. There was nothing to catch hold of, so they held tight, each to the other, and went like projectiles down the icy slope, head first, into a deep soft bed of snow. Ezekiel Crofton's Newfoundland dog was on the spot as their heads disappeared, and then nothing was visible for a moment but his huge black skin and the doctor's boots and one leg of the minister, at which the dog was tugging as if to save a drowning man.

So ended, and ended joyously, too, the merciful errand of that night. For the doctor, when he entered the sick-room, found Susie in a wild excitement, and her mother sitting up in bed laughing, and out of danger. I don't know what the doctor called the disease of which she was supposed to be dying. It was some trouble of the throat. She had been lying with her face towards the window, gasping. Even in the hour of death, when she was looking into the light as of the last earthly morning, the scene had overpowered all sense of solemnity, and the burst of laughter had removed the trouble which was killing her.

It might do you good, once in a while these winter nights, when you wake warm and comfortable in your city bed, to think what possible errands men like those two may just then be out on in the up country.

XX

HINTS FOR CARRIAGE TRAVEL

FIRST, as to horses. There is a common idea that heavy horses are not as good travellers as lighter animals. This does not accord with my experience in really working-horses. For a spurt, or a day or two of hard driving, it may well be that light horses will go faster and come in less worried than heavier animals. But for continuous travelling, with a reasonably heavy load, day after day, taking any and every kind of road, ascending and descending hills and mountains, it is my opinion after long experience that strong, heavy horses are more trustworthy and useful, do their work with less fatigue, and do it better. My black horses, Ned and Jack, now grown old and living in almost inglorious idleness, weigh twelve hundred and fifty each. I have a pair of grays that weigh short twelve hundred each. My carriage with my regular travel load weighs a trifle under fourteen hundred. Either pair of horses will take us along on roads up hill and down at an average gait of five miles to the hour. This is fast enough for one to drive who travels to see everything that is to be seen on both sides of the road. It may happen, after a day of loitering along, that I find myself towards evening eight or ten miles from my proposed resting-place. My horses can do that in an hour, and come in in good order. I seldom average over twenty-five miles a day. But, on occasion, I drive forty-five miles a day, without fatigue to these horses. Few light horses can be depended on for such little afternoon spurts, or such extra days, over rough or mountainous roads, on a journey of four or five hundred miles, with three-fourths of a ton behind them.

A comfortable carriage, comfortable for both horses and travellers, is a very rare object in our day. The tendency of late years has been to build carriages to be looked at, or to show off the persons and dresses of the occupants. With this has grown the fashion of building carriages with narrow box seats, into which two persons can crowd side by side only by wedging as they take their seats.

In carriage travel the primary considerations for the vehicle are strength and *roominess*. Don't save a hundred or two pounds of weight at the expense of strength. Get horses that will draw your load, and don't sacrifice safety and sureness. By sureness, I mean this: that a break-down in a lonesome road, miles from a blacksmith, is an unpleasant accident.

Breadth of beam is what you need to give room.

Your running-gear must be of the ordinary gauge in use in the country you travel in, and your carriage-box as wide as possible on that gear. The seats should be so wide that two persons can sit on them with room between them for a book, or a small bag, or any little traps. The front and back seat should be on a level. I generally travel with three in the carriage, one on the back seat, myself and coachman on the front seat. This leaves ample room on the back seat and bottom for books, maps, flowers that we gather, wraps, and the small impedimenta of travel; while a rack behind the carriage holds the trunks, which are not heavy, but with their leverage power balance the weight of two on the front seat and make even springs. It is well that the carriage top be an ordinary extension top, reaching forward over the front seat, which can be thrown completely back and lie on the baggage. In soft October days there is vast delight in riding in the sunshine.

To those who travel for the enjoyments which we desire, it is objectionable to have a carriage door. The side should present no impediment to frequent stepping out and in, and the footsteps should be broad and roughened. You see a flower, a bunch of moss, a stone; innumerable objects along the road-side attract your eye; and you get out scores of times and get in again with your treasure. As the day passes you accumulate a heap of such things that you have examined and talked about after gathering. Towards evening, as you approach your resting-place, out they go on the road-side. Two-thirds of the pleasure and profit of this travel is in thus getting out of the carriage, sometimes for only an instant.

Going up or down hill I often stop, for the reason that I have a *brake*. I italicize the word because it is so absolutely essential to the comfort and safety of both travellers and horses. It is marvellous that in ordinary hilly country so few persons have brakes on their pleasure carriages, buggies, or business wagons. One can be easily attached to any vehicle by any blacksmith, and will add years to the healthy life of your horses. No trouble is more common with horses than lameness in the fore-legs or shoulders. This comes, in countless instances, from trotting downhill with a load behind. The horse is not free in action. If he were at perfect liberty he would go lightly, set his feet down with instinctive certainty and without pounding. But he has a load, pulling by traces on his fore-shoulders, jerking pulls, now following fast on him, now brought up suddenly by a stone or a water-bar. No horse thus encumbered can trot downhill without constant danger of pounding his fore-feet heavily down, producing a strain in the shoulder, perhaps twisting his leg or ankle when his foot goes down on a stone, or somewhere where he does not mean to put it. So, too, the strain of holding back a heavy load, with the breeching around the thighs, produces the same effects. Of course no one will be guilty of trying northern travel with a light harness and no breechings.

I repeat, for the benefit of all the race of carriage horses, as well as for the benefit of those who own and value horses, that in a hilly country every buggy, wagon, and carriage should be provided with a brake. It is hardly necessary to add that for the pleasure-traveller, who wants to stop anywhere along the road-side, it is indispensable. In western Massachusetts and Connecticut, Vermont, and New Hampshire, a steady uphill grade of two or three miles is a common feature of roads, and it is not uncommon to find a mountain pass where the road is uphill for six, eight, or ten miles. If one desires a glorious ride, let him drive from Westfield in Massachusetts to Norfolk in Connecticut, and learn how to ascend and descend hills for the sake of every variety of scenery. But if he try that country without strong horses, a stout carriage, and a safe brake, he will chance to come to grief, with no help in sight.

Look well to the bolts which attach the pole and hauling-gear to your carriage. Many carriage-builders neglect this. A heavy carriage, with abundant iron-work, warranted strong, will often be found drawn by two small iron bolts in thin rings, both of which are daily wearing weaker. Reinforce iron-work with straps. Iron is poor stuff to depend on; "there's nothing like leather." Have a strong neck-yoke or strong hold-back on the end of your pole. A brake saves danger there, but you cannot be too safe. Don't forego safety for the sake of beauty. Travel to look, not to be looked at.

Don't trust your horses to the attention of hostlers, but when you reach a resting-place, secure their comfort for the night before you secure your own. If you love your horses as I love mine, you will need no such advice. When you start in the morning take a thorough look over your harness and carriage, to see that all is right for the road. Talk a little while with the horses before you start, chat with them once in a while along the road, especially if you happen to be walking uphill beside them or before them, and always make sure to speak with them when the day's work is done.

Cleanliness prevails in north-country inns. In an experience of thousands of miles of travel along New England roads, during many years, my notebook records only three or four instances where I was compelled to write "not clean" of the inn in which I passed the night. Food is abundant everywhere and of the best quality. Good bread, and milk, fresh eggs, fruits, vegetables, preserved or cooked fruits, cake made in great variety—these are found on every table. There has been in former years a universal idea that beefsteak was essential to a traveller's supper and breakfast. Country-killed beef, however good in flavor, is generally very tough and hard. The certainty of the appearance of this tough beefsteak has led me to adopt the custom of saying when I enter an inn, "Don't give us any beef." I recommend the traveller by carriage to follow my example. I have never found in Europe or America finer mutton or lamb than is abundant with us all along our drives. You should carry your own tea and coffee.

The roads are fairly good, but we notice, especially in Vermont, a manifest deterioration from year to year in their character. They are growing poorer, and this is perhaps due to the fact that the towns are growing poorer.

The whole system of road-making by town-tax is bad. It is not to be expected that a poor town, which happens to lie on a route of travel between two or more populous towns, should keep up first-class roads for the use of those who pay nothing towards them. Nor do people with whom road making and repairing is a matter of annual taxation take any personal interest or have any personal pride in their roads. The worst mud holes in roads are frequently in front of good farmhouses. It would take the farmer an hour, with his horses, to fill up such a hole and make a good road by his front door. But that would be doing work which is the town's business to do, and he would get no pay for it; so he lets it alone. If he is drawing a heavy load uphill he chocks his wheels with a stone to rest his horses, and drives on, leaving the stone in the road. To throw it out, and to throw out other stones left by other teamsters, would be doing town work, and he will not do that in his own town, much less in another town.

Do you know what is meant by "working out the road-tax?" Each man's proportion of work is assessed. He has so many days' work to pay. The times of working on roads are fixed by the town officer. Carts, horses, ploughs, etc., are furnished on order, and allowed for at fixed rates. You have seen the deliberate slowness with which day-laborers on railways, or on contract work in city streets, perform their labor. These men are lively and swift compared with the country farmer when working out his road-tax. The gravel-bed is perhaps a half-mile down the road. Four or five men with shovels load a cart there in three minutes, and having loaded it, sit down and smoke and chat a half-hour till it returns empty. Down on the roadway four or five men await the cart, smoking and chatting, dump and spread the dirt or gravel when it comes, taking three minutes for the job, and smoke and chat a half-hour till the cart comes again. If they planted and gathered crops as they make roads, they would starve. It is not because they are lazy or indolent. These are men of might in their own affairs. But they are working out the road-tax, and who ever heard that a man ought to work in payment of a tax as he works for himself?

It is rarely necessary to drive anywhere in Vermont or New Hampshire more than ten or fifteen miles to find a good inn. Whether going north, south, east, or west, it is usually practicable to ride pleasantly in the forenoon for two or three hours, stop at noon to feed the horses and get luncheon, which will be called dinner, drive again two, three, or four hours in the afternoon and strike a comfortable inn for supper and night-lodging. Day's drives can thus be adjusted according to your pleasure. You will linger in pleasant places; you will loiter along some roads; you will change your preconceived route suddenly, at noon, or in the morning, or along the road. Sometimes you will drive only a few miles. At other times you may be induced to press your horses to their extreme ability in order to reach a desired resting-place. But I recommend you to regard your horses and do not give them hard days' works. Let them enjoy the travel as you enjoy it. You may have great confidence in the health and strength of your horses, but do not forget that for horses as for men, travelling, eating in various places, spending nights in various stables, drinking varieties of water, subjected to various weather exposures, all this is very different from home life. Oats vary as much as bread varies. Hay is a very variable food. Men will assure you in October that they have only old oats, and sicken your horses by giving them grain threshed three weeks ago, unless you watch them; and it is by no means easy to tell new oats from old. For comfort and enjoyment an average of twenty-five miles a day is quite enough for you or your horses. If you enjoy the country, with its innumerable beauties, you will often be content with five miles, and constantly desire to remain just where you are.

Finally, don't be in a hurry, and when you start out for the day's drive do not start with the determination to go to a certain place. That is not what you are taking a carriage journey for. You may and will fix on a place as a probable end of your day, but don't go off in the morning with mind set on reaching there as the day's purpose. Loiter along; stroll in the woods; sit awhile on a rock by the side of a lake; stop long on the hilltops and take in the glory of American scenery. If you are an angler, your rod, unjointed but ready with line, leader, and flies, lies fore-and-aft on your carriage seats, and many a brook or pond or lake, in the spring-time, will pay you for a cast. In the autumn your gun lies ready, and partridges crossing the road will tempt you often out of your carriage. You will not get many, but you will have all the excitement, and may now and then carry your supper or breakfast in with you.

THE END